THE KINGFISHER
Children's
ATLAS

KINGFISHER

KINGFISHER

Kingfisher Publications Plc
New Penderel House
283–288 High Holborn
London WC1V 7HZ
www.kingfisherpub.com

Written by
Belinda Weber

Senior editor: Catherine Brereton
Art director: Mike Davis
Designer: Anthony Cutting
Assistant designer: Chloe Aylward
Cartographic consultant: Jan Clark
Picture researcher: Rachael Swann
DTP co-ordinator: Jonathan Pledge
Senior production controller: Lindsey Scott
Artwork archivists: Wendy Allison, Jenny Lord
Proof-reader: Sheila Clewley
Indexer: Jan Clark
Additional research: Mike Davis
Cover designed by: Mike Davis

Cartography by: Anderson Geographics Limited,
Warfield, Berkshire

First published by Kingfisher Publications Plc 2004
3 5 7 9 10 8 6 4 2
2TR/0806/SHEN/CLSN(CLSN)/128MA/F

A CIP catalogue record for this book is available from the British Library.

ISBN-13: 978 0 7534 0960 2
ISBN-10: 0 7534 0960 7
Printed in Taiwan

CONTENTS

THE EARTH

The Earth is a planet that rotates around the Sun. It is covered by huge land masses, called continents, and vast oceans and seas. There are seven continents: North America, South America, Europe, Africa, Asia, Australasia and Oceania, and Antarctica. Most of them have a variety of different types of landscape. There are high, mountainous regions and low-lying plains. Where there is little or no rain, deserts are found. Flowing rivers can bring an abundance of animal and plant life to an area, and also cut paths through the landscape. In areas with high rainfall, rainforests can grow, providing lush green oases.

Humans also influence the landscape. We farm the land and build villages, towns and huge cities with skyscrapers for people to live and work in.

Shaping the world

Humans also shape the landscape by dividing the land into countries. Some countries are whole islands, but most are parts of the larger land masses. Often, mountains or rivers mark the boundaries between countries, but sometimes there is nothing physical to mark the border where one country ends and another begins. Humans live on almost every bit of land on the planet. At present, there are around 6,343 million people living in the world.

Mountain ranges
Mountains reach high towards the sky. The higher they are, the colder the temperature. Very few animals can live at the tops.

Sandy deserts
In places with little or no rain, deserts, such as the Sahara, form. This sandy wilderness covers much of Northern Africa.

Winding rivers
Rivers and streams wind their way through the landscape on their way to the sea. They can carve paths through solid rock.

Green and wet
Tropical rainforests grow in hot, rainy areas, carpeting the land with a rich variety of plant life. Animals thrive in these forests.

Maps and mapping

We use maps and globes to show and find out about the countries of the world. A globe is a ball with all the continents and oceans drawn on it. A map is a flat plan of the world. Imagine that you had an orange with all the countries and seas drawn on it. If you peeled it and laid the peel out flat, you would not get a complete oblong. Map-makers make a whole picture by stretching the shape of some countries and seas. Map-makers also draw imaginary lines across the Earth's surface. Lines around the Earth are called lines of latitude. Lines going top to bottom are called lines of longitude. These form a grid over the Earth's surface, which help us pinpoint exactly where in the world a place is.

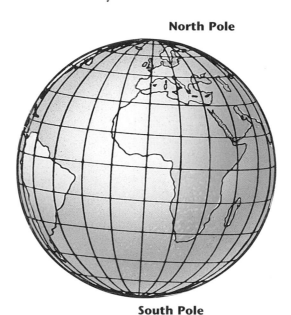

North Pole

South Pole

Pole to pole
Lines going from top to bottom are called lines of longitude. All the lines of longitude meet at the North and South Poles, which are the most northerly and southerly points on Earth.

Greenwich meridian
The line of longitude in the middle of the Earth is called the Greenwich meridian.

Equator
Lines around the Earth are called lines of latitude. The equator is a line of latitude around the middle of the Earth.

Concrete jungles
Humans build huge cities to house millions of people. These urban buildings change the look of a once natural landscape.

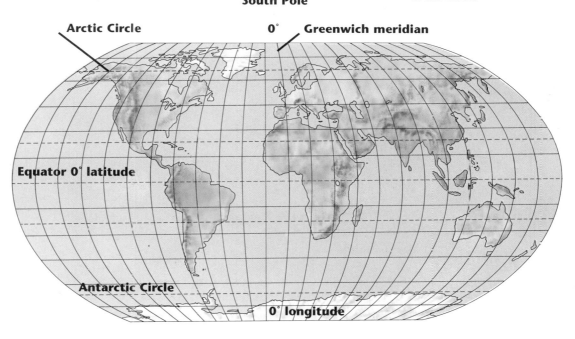

Arctic Circle   0°   Greenwich meridian

Equator 0° latitude

Antarctic Circle

0° longitude

Using maps

An atlas is a book of maps. Maps are pictures that tell us about different places. They provide all sorts of useful information about countries. Maps use different colours, symbols and lines to show mountains and valleys, oceans and seas, and rivers and lakes. On most of the maps in this atlas, like the example below, colours are also used to show the height of the land above sea level. Some maps use colours to show different kinds of information, such as where there are fertile places and deserts.

Red lines on the maps show where one country starts and another ends. These lines are called borders. Squares represent capital cities. A capital is the main city in a country, where the government and other important organizations are based. A few countries have more than one capital. All other towns and cities on the maps are marked with red dots. The maps in this atlas also have picture symbols which show you where to find animals, industry, landmarks and a variety of places of interest.

The maps in this atlas use a set group of symbols and words to mark various different types of features. This key shows you what they all mean.

Settlements

- ■ CARACAS   Capital city
- ■ Denver   State capital city
- ● Manaus   Major city or town
- • Maturín   Other city or town

Political and cultural regions

BRAZIL   Country

Aruba   Dependent territory
(to Netherlands)

ARIZONA   State, province or national region

Boundaries

　　　　　International border
- - - - - - Disputed border
　　　　　State, province or national regional boundary

Drainage features

　　　　　River
- - - - - Seasonal river
　　　　　Canal
　　　　　Waterfall
　　　　　Lake
　　　　　Seasonal lake

Topographic features

△ *Cotopaxi 5,897 m*   Height of mountain

Isla de Marájo   Island / island group

Amazon Basin   Physical feature / landscape region

Seas and oceans

PACIFIC OCEAN   Name of ocean

Caribbean Sea   Name of sea

   Sea

Ice features

   Limit of summer pack ice
　　　　　Limit of winter pack ice

Land height

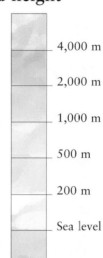

- 4,000 m
- 2,000 m
- 1,000 m
- 500 m
- 200 m
- Sea level

Extra information

Alongside the maps, you will find symbols telling you more about the area covered by the map, to help you understand where it fits in the world.

Flags
Every country in the world has its own national flag. You will find these flags throughout the atlas. They symbolize the country's independence and identity.

Globe
The globe on each page shows (marked in orange) where the countries on the map are in the world. Some of the map pages have an extra map in a small box, called an inset. The position of these is shown by an orange box on the globe.

Scale bar
All the maps in this atlas have a scale bar. This will tell you how distances on the page relate to real distances on the ground. For example, the scale bar shown below tells you that 28 mm on the map represents 500 km on the ground.

A　　　　　　　B

Grid
Around the edges of each page you will find a grid with letters and numbers. The index at the end of the book will give you a page number and grid reference. By using the grid reference, you will be able to find the particular town or city you are looking for.

Picture symbols

On the maps, you will also find picture symbols which show interesting features in each country. Here are a few examples. Look out for more throughout the atlas.

Cattle
An example of a farm animal

Fishing
An example of a type of industry

Toucan
An example of a kind of wildlife

Catedral Basílica
An example of a famous building or landmark

Bananas
An example of a food crop

Countries of the world

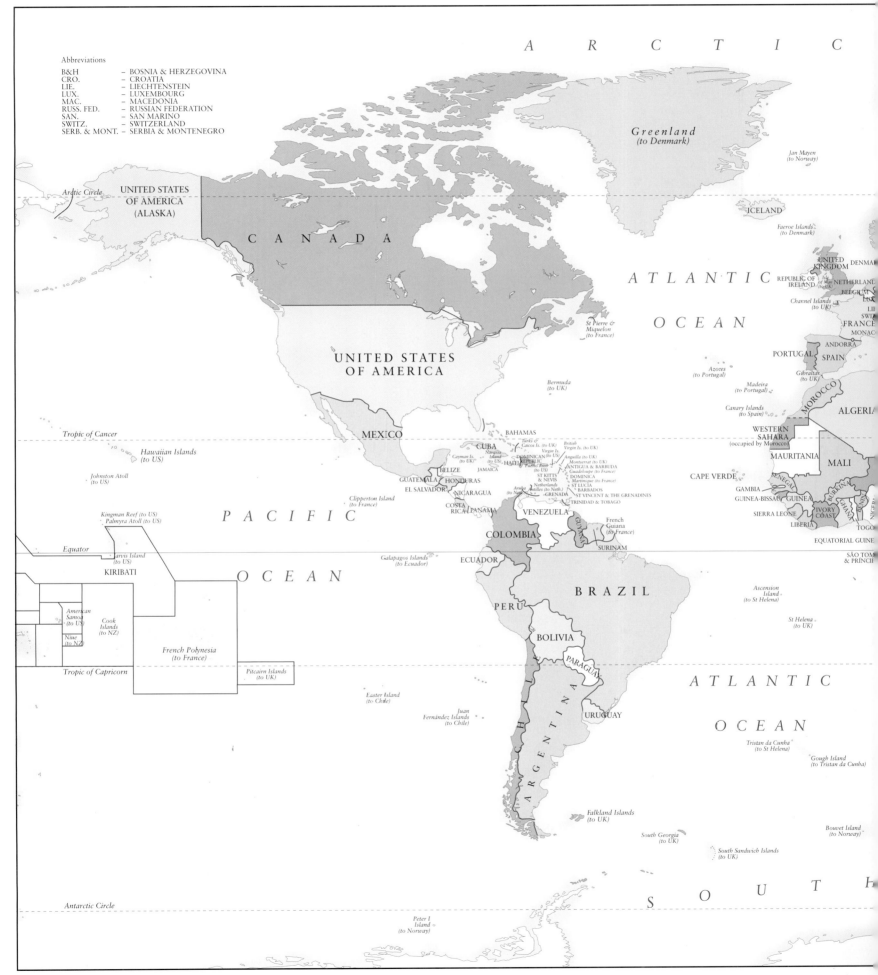

ARCTIC

Greenland
(to Denmark)

Jan Mayen
(to Norway)

Arctic Circle

UNITED STATES
OF AMERICA
(ALASKA)

CANADA

ICELAND

Faeroe Islands
(to Denmark)

ATLANTIC

UNITED
KINGDOM   DENMARK

REPUBLIC OF   NETHERLANDS
IRELAND   BELGIUM

OCEAN   Channel Islands   LUX.
               (to UK)   LIE.
                                  SWITZ.
St Pierre &   FRANCE
Miquelon   MONACO
(to France)
                         ANDORRA

UNITED STATES   PORTUGAL   SPAIN
OF AMERICA

Bermuda   Azores   MOROCCO
(to UK)   (to Portugal)

                       Madeira   ALGERIA
Tropic of Cancer   (to Portugal)

MEXICO   BAHAMAS   Canary Islands   WESTERN
Hawaiian Islands   (to Spain)   SAHARA
(to US)   (occupied by Morocco)
             CUBA   Turks &   MAURITANIA   MALI
Johnston Atoll   Caicos Is. (to UK)   British
(to US)   Nassau   DOMINICAN Virgin Is. (to UK)
             Cayman Is. Island REPUBLIC   Anguilla (to UK)   CAPE VERDE
             (to UK)   JAMAICA HAITI Puerto Rico ANTIGUA & BARBUDA
                       BELIZE   (to US) DOMINICA
Kingman Reef (to US) GUATEMALA HONDURAS ST KITTS Guadeloupe (to France)
Palmyra Atoll (to US) EL SALVADOR & NEVIS Martinique (to France)   SENEGAL
                                            ST LUCIA   GAMBIA
             NICARAGUA Aruba Netherlands BARBADOS   GUINEA-BISSAU GUINEA
Equator   (to Neth.) Antilles ST VINCENT & THE GRENADINES
Jarvis Island   COSTA (to Neth.) GRENADA SIERRA LEONE   IVORY
(to US)   RICA PANAMA TRINIDAD & TOBAGO   LIBERIA COAST
KIRIBATI   VENEZUELA   French   EQUATORIAL GUINE
                                                Guiana
                                 COLOMBIA GUYANA (to France)   SÃO TOM
                   Galapagos Islands   SURINAM   & PRINCI
                   (to Ecuador)   ECUADOR
American   Ascension
Samoa   Cook   BRAZIL   Island
(to US)   Islands   (to St Helena)
          (to NZ)   PERU
Niue
(to NZ)   BOLIVIA   St Helena
          French   (to UK)
          Polynesia   PARAGUAY
Tropic of Capricorn (to France)
                   Pitcairn Islands
                   (to UK)   ATLANTIC
           Easter Island
           (to Chile)
Juan   OCEAN
Fernández Islands   URUGUAY
(to Chile)
                                            Tristan da Cunha
                                            (to St Helena)
                                                  Gough Island
                                                  (to Tristan da Cunha)
                       ARGENTINA

                                   Falkland Islands
                                   (to UK)   Bouvet Island
                                  South Georgia   (to Norway)
                                  (to UK)
                                        South Sandwich Islands
                                        (to UK)

                                                   SOUTH

Antarctic Circle

Peter I
Island
(to Norway)

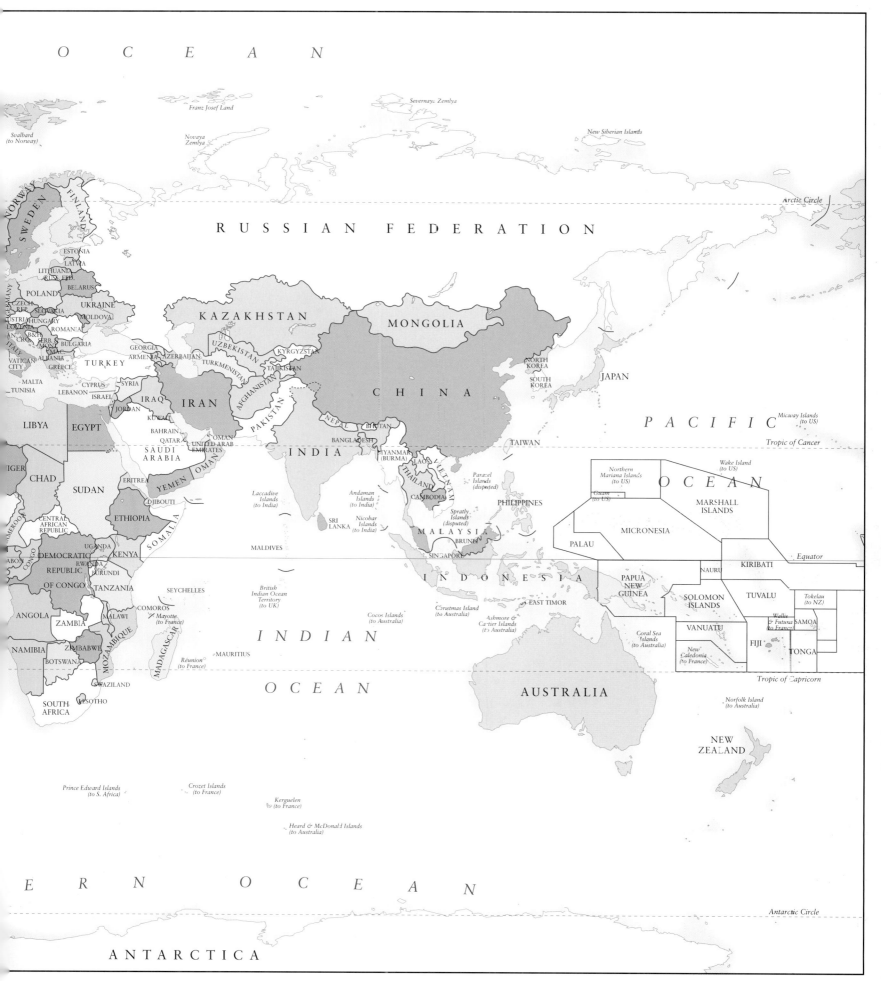

OCEAN

Franz Josef Land

Svalbard (to Norway)

Novaya Zemlya

Severnaya Zemlya

New Siberian Islands

RUSSIAN FEDERATION

NORWAY
SWEDEN
FINLAND
ESTONIA
LATVIA
LITHUANIA
RUS. FED.
BELARUS
POLAND
UKRAINE
CZECH REP.
SLOVAKIA
AUSTRIA
HUNGARY
MOLDOVA
SLOVENIA
CRO.
B.&H.
SERB. & MONT.
ROMANIA
ITALY
VATICAN CITY
ALBANIA
BULGARIA
GREECE
MALTA
TUNISIA
CYPRUS
LEBANON
ISRAEL
SYRIA
TURKEY
GEORGIA
ARMENIA
AZERBAIJAN

KAZAKHSTAN

MONGOLIA

UZBEKISTAN
KYRGYZSTAN
TURKMENISTAN
TAJIKISTAN
AFGHANISTAN

NORTH KOREA
SOUTH KOREA

JAPAN

CHINA

IRAQ
IRAN
JORDAN
KUWAIT
BAHRAIN
QATAR
UNITED ARAB EMIRATES
OMAN
SAUDI ARABIA

PAKISTAN

NEPAL
BHUTAN

TAIWAN

PACIFIC

Midway Islands (to US)

LIBYA
EGYPT

NIGER
CHAD
SUDAN
ERITREA
YEMEN
DJIBOUTI
ETHIOPIA
SOMALIA

CAMEROON
CENTRAL AFRICAN REPUBLIC
UGANDA
KENYA
GABON
CONGO
DEMOCRATIC REPUBLIC OF CONGO
RWANDA
BURUNDI
TANZANIA

INDIA

BANGLADESH
MYANMAR (BURMA)
LAOS
VIETNAM
THAILAND
CAMBODIA

Laccadive Islands (to India)

Andaman Islands (to India)

Paracel Islands (disputed)

PHILIPPINES

Nicobar Islands (to India)

SRI LANKA

MALDIVES

Spratly Islands (disputed)

MALAYSIA
BRUNEI
SINGAPORE

OCEAN

Northern Mariana Islands (to US)

Guam (to US)

MARSHALL ISLANDS

MICRONESIA

PALAU

NAURU

KIRIBATI

Wake Island (to US)

SEYCHELLES

COMOROS
Mayotte (to France)

MALAWI

ANGOLA
ZAMBIA

NAMIBIA
ZIMBABWE
BOTSWANA
MOZAMBIQUE

British Indian Ocean Territory (to UK)

Cocos Islands (to Australia)

Christmas Island (to Australia)

INDONESIA

EAST TIMOR

Ashmore & Cartier Islands (to Australia)

PAPUA NEW GUINEA

SOLOMON ISLANDS

Coral Sea Islands (to Australia)

VANUATU

New Caledonia (to France)

TUVALU

Tokelau (to NZ)

Wallis & Futuna (to France)

FIJI

SAMOA

TONGA

INDIAN

MADAGASCAR
Réunion (to France)
MAURITIUS

SOUTH AFRICA
LESOTHO
SWAZILAND

OCEAN

AUSTRALIA

Norfolk Island (to Australia)

Prince Edward Islands (to S. Africa)

Crozet Islands (to France)

Kerguelen (to France)

Heard & McDonald Islands (to Australia)

NEW ZEALAND

ERN OCEAN

ANTARCTICA

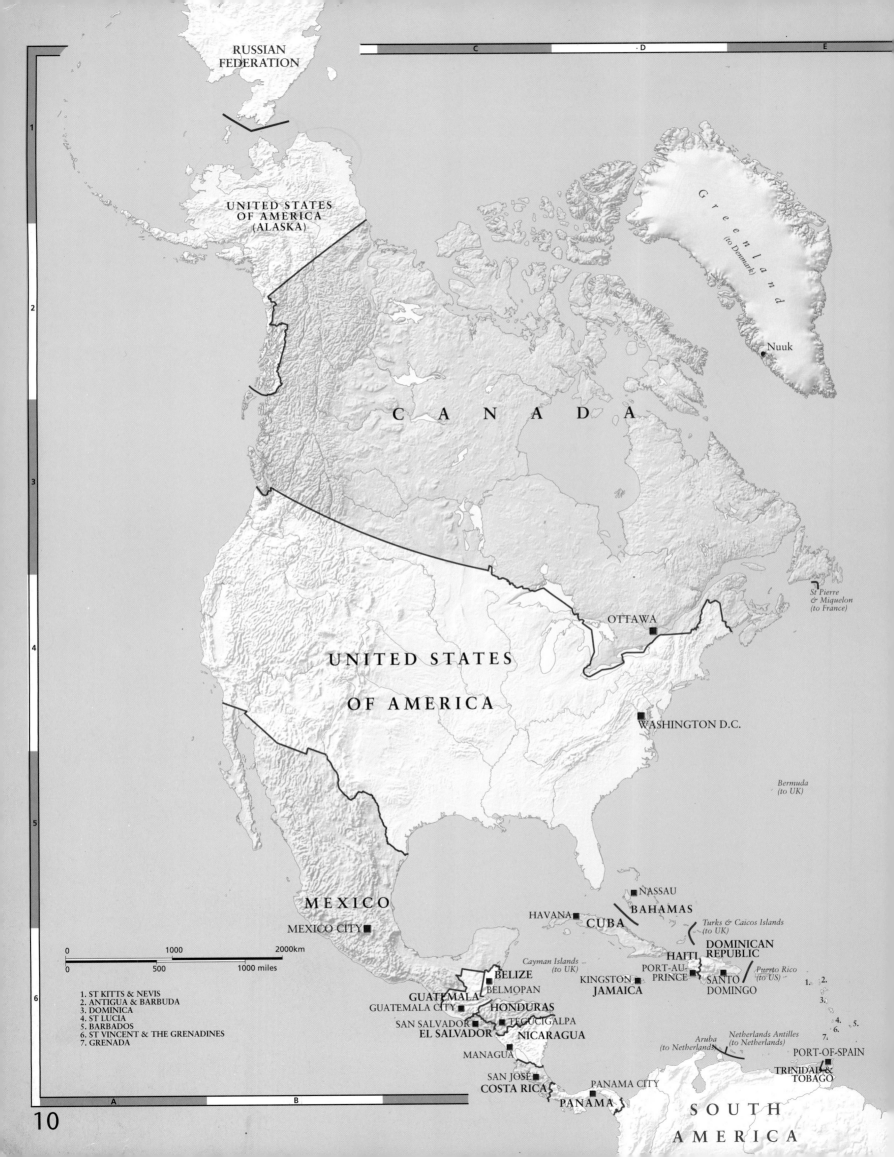

RUSSIAN
FEDERATION

UNITED STATES
OF AMERICA
(ALASKA)

G r e e n l a n d
(to Denmark)

C A N A D A

• Nuuk

St Pierre
& Miquelon
(to France)

OTTAWA ■

UNITED STATES

OF AMERICA

WASHINGTON D.C. ■

Bermuda
(to UK)

■ NASSAU

MEXICO

HAVANA ■ CUBA BAHAMAS

Turks & Caicos Islands
(to UK)

MEXICO CITY ■

Cayman Islands
(to UK)

DOMINICAN
REPUBLIC

HAITI

BELIZE
■ BELMOPAN

PORT-AU-
PRINCE ■ SANTO
DOMINGO

Puerto Rico
(to US)

KINGSTON ■
JAMAICA

1.   2.

3.

GUATEMALA
GUATEMALA CITY ■ HONDURAS
SAN SALVADOR ■ ■ TEGUCIGALPA
EL SALVADOR NICARAGUA

4.   5.
6.

Aruba
(to Netherlands)

Netherlands Antilles
(to Netherlands)

7.

■ MANAGUA

PORT-OF-SPAIN ■

SAN JOSÉ ■ PANAMA CITY ■
COSTA RICA

TRINIDAD &
TOBAGO

PANAMA ■

S O U T H

A M E R I C A

1. ST KITTS & NEVIS
2. ANTIGUA & BARBUDA
3. DOMINICA
4. ST LUCIA
5. BARBADOS
6. ST VINCENT & THE GRENADINES
7. GRENADA

0		1000		2000km
0	500		1000 miles	

Rich farmland
The Mississippi river carries sediment (tiny specks of mud) in its waters which it leaves as fertile soil along its way. Many crops are grown on the plains beside the river.

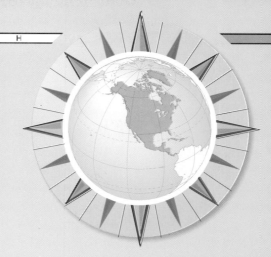

NORTH AMERICA

The continent of North America is the third largest continent. It stretches from the frozen Arctic in the north to the tropics in the south. In winter, the far north is bitterly cold as icy winds blow off the Arctic. Most parts of the continent have warm or hot summers. The Rocky Mountains stretch down the west of the continent, reaching from the north of Canada to Mexico. On the east of the continent lie the Appalachians, and in between these two mountain ranges are large flat plains, across which the mighty Mississippi and Missouri rivers flow.

North America consists of three large countries: Canada, the United States of America and Mexico; as well as the island of Greenland and the smaller countries of Central America and the Caribbean.

Crystal clear
Canada has more lakes and inland water than anywhere else in the world. Many national parks have been set up to protect the lakes and the areas surrounding them.

Thumbs up!
People from many different cultures make up the United States of America. Settlers from Europe, Africa and Asia as well as the native Americans are all part of a multicultural society.

Canada

Canada is an enormous country – the second largest in the world after the Russian Federation. Yet most of Canada's 30 million people live in the south, in cities along the border with the United States. Very few people live in the Northwest Territories, or in the islands off the north, as the lands here are inside the Arctic Circle and temperatures can drop to a bitterly cold -40°C. The Rocky Mountains in the west are covered with trees, and are home to wildlife such as the bald eagle. In the far north, there are polar bears. In the central areas are vast plains, where large quantities of wheat are grown.

Half of Canada's population live along the St Lawrence Seaway, near the Great Lakes. Canada has two official languages – French and English. Most of the French-speaking Canadians live in the province of Québec.

Long journey
Monarch butterflies from Canada gather in their thousands each autumn and fly south. They spend the winter in Florida, southern California and northern Mexico. Some travel over 3,430 km.

FACTS AND FIGURES

Largest cities
Toronto 4,683,000
Montreal 3,426,000

Longest river
Mackenzie 1,733 km

Largest lake
Lake Superior 82,350 km². This is the largest lake in North America and the second largest in the world

Highest mountain
Mount Logan 5,959 m

ARCTIC OCEAN

Beaufort Sea

Polar bear

Ice breaker

Banks Island

Victoria Island

Amundsen Gulf

UNITED STATES OF AMERICA (ALASKA)

Oil

Snowshoe hare

Arctic Circle

Arctic fox

Musk ox

YUKON TERRITORY

Mount Logan 5,959 m

Mount Vancouver 4,785 m

Whitehorse

Mining

Mackenzie Mountains

Mackenzie

NORTHWEST TERRITORIES

Great Bear Lake

Yellowknife

Great Slave Lake

Slave

Bald eagle

Alexander Archipelago

Coast Mountains

Brown bear

Caribou Mountains

Peace

Birch Mountains

Lake Athabasca

Pacific salmon

Prince Rupert

Queen Charlotte Islands

BRITISH COLUMBIA

Gas

Skiing

C A

SASKATCHEW

Monarch butterfly

Prince George

Rocky Mountains

ALBERTA

Oil

Edmonton

N. Saskatchewan

Great Plains

Mount Waddington 4,016 m

Athabasca

Coal mining

S. Saskatchewan

Vancouver Island

Fraser

Totem pole

Industry

Calgary

Saskatoon

Vancouver

Victoria

Medicine Hat

Regina

PACIFIC OCEAN

Wheat farming

0   500   1000 km
0   250   500 miles

UNITED STATES OF AMERICA

Ellesmere
Island

Axel
Heiburg
Island

Queen
Elizabeth
Islands

Melville
Island

Parry
Islands

Devon Island

Viscount Melville
Sound

Lancaster Sound

McClintock

Somerset
Island

Prince
of Wales
Island

Gulf
of
Boothia

Boothia
Peninsula

Channel

Melville
Peninsula

Prince
Charles
Island

Nettilling
Lake

Foxe
Basin

Amadjuak
Lake

G r e e n l a n d
(to Denmark)

B a f f i n
B a y

Ringed seal

Narwhal

Baffin Island

Davis Strait

Arctic Circle

Iqaluit

Labrador
Sea

Fast and furious

Ice hockey is Canada's most
popular sport. This high-
speed game was first played
on the frozen waters of
Kingston harbour, Ontario,
around 1860CE.

Wolf

Inuit people

Snowplough

Caribou

Dubawnt
Lake

N U N A V U T

Southampton
Island

Hudson Strait

Cape Chidley

Canada
goose

Ungava
Bay

A T L A N T I C

O C E A N

Beluga

Ungava
Peninsula

Labrador

Wolverine

Hudson
Bay

Mining

NEWFOUNDLAND
& LABRADOR

Canada

Wollaston
Lake

Reindeer
Lake

Churchill

Nelson

Canadian

Belcher
Islands

Mining

Smallwood
Reservoir

Newfoundland

St John's

Cape
Race

Granville
Lake

Wheat

Lake
Winnipegosis

MANITOBA

Beaver

James
Bay

QUÉBEC

Manicouagan
Reservoir

Laurentian Highlands

Gulf of
St Lawrence

St Pierre
& Miquelon
(to France)

Lake
Manitoba

Lake
Winnipeg

Ice hockey

Logging

Woodchuck

Paper making

Computers

St Lawrence

Cape Breton
Island

PRINCE
EDWARD
ISLAND

NEW
BRUNSWICK

Charlottetown

NOVA
SCOTIA

Industry

Winnipeg

Thunder Bay

Lake of
the Woods

O N T A R I O

Mining

Lake
Nipigon

Gold mining

Shield

Québec

Parliament

Fredericton

St John

Halifax

OTTAWA

Montreal

Bay of Fundy

Cape Sable

Cod

CN Tower

Kingston

Sault Ste Marie

Sudbury

Lake
Superior

Georgian
Bay

Industry

Lake Ontario

Fishing

Lake
Huron

Toronto

Lake
Michigan

Hamilton

London

Industry

Lake
Erie

Niagara Falls

Western United States

The United States of America occupies the central part of the continent of North America. This powerful country is divided into 50 states. The land and climate across such a huge country varies greatly, from icy Arctic wilderness in Alaska to burning hot deserts in Arizona, swamps in the Everglades, and rolling grasslands in the prairies of the mid-west.

The western USA includes landmarks such as the Grand Canyon, a deep gorge carved out by the Colorado river. In California, the climate is perfect for orange-growing. It is also the home of Silicon Valley, where microchips and electronic devices are produced.

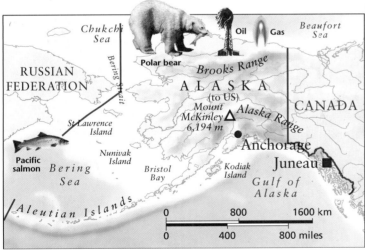

Strait of Juan de Fuca
Cape Flattery
Aircraft manufacturing
Mount Olympus 2,428 m
Seattle
WASHINGTON
Spokane
Olympia
Apples
Columbia Basin
Mount Rainier 4,392 m
Columbia
Snake
Mount Saint Helens 2,549 m
Portland
Columbia
Clearwater Mountains
Salem
Blue Mountains
Salmon Range
Bitterroot Range
Fishing
Eugene
Timber production
IDAHO
Sheep
Salmon River Mountains
Cascade Range
OREGON
Potatoes
Golden eagle
Boise
Malheur Lake
Columbia Plateau
Snake
Giant redwood
Brown bear
U N I
Coast Ranges
Mount Shasta 4,316 m
Pit
Brown bear
Gold mining
Humboldt
Great Salt Lake
Cape Mendocino
Wine
Gold mining
Pyramid Lake
Kit fox
Great Salt Lake Desert
Golden Gate Bridge
Sacramento
Reno
Carson City
G r e a t
Cop min
San Francisco
Lake Tahoe
Sacramento
NEVADA
Sevier Lake
San Jose
Monterey Bay
Electronics (Silicon Valley)
Grapes
B a s i n
Casinos
UT
Colo
A
Fresno
Rattlesnake
Mount Whitney 4,418 m
Sierra Nevada
Death Valley
CALIFORNIA
Las Vegas
Lake Mead
Grand Canyon
Pla
Sealion
Hoover Dam
Point Conception
Oranges
Mojave Desert
Grand Canyon
Hollywood
Los Angeles
Desert tortoise
ARIZONA
PACIFIC
Colorado
Phoenix
OCEAN
San Diego
Salton Sea
Gila
Sonoran Desert
Tucson
Gila monster

Chukchi Sea
Oil
Gas
Beaufort Sea
Polar bear
Brooks Range
RUSSIAN FEDERATION
ALASKA (to US)
CANADA
Bering Strait
St Lawrence Island
Mount McKinley 6,194 m
Alaska Range
Pacific salmon
Nunivak Island
Bristol Bay
Kodiak Island
Anchorage
Juneau
Bering Sea
Gulf of Alaska
Aleutian Islands

0		800	1600 km
0	400	800 miles	

Kauai
0 — 200 km
0 — 100 miles
Oahu
Honolulu
Molokai
H A W A I I (to US)
Surfing
Maui
Red Hill 3,055 m
Mauna Kea 4,205 m
Hawaii
Mauna Loa 4,169 m
Pineapple
PACIFIC OCEAN

FACTS AND FIGURES

Largest cities
Los Angeles 12,745,000
Dallas 5,484,000

Largest state
Alaska

Longest river
Mississippi-Missouri 6,020 km

Highest mountain
Mount McKinley 6,194 m

Lowest point
Death Valley 86 m below sea level

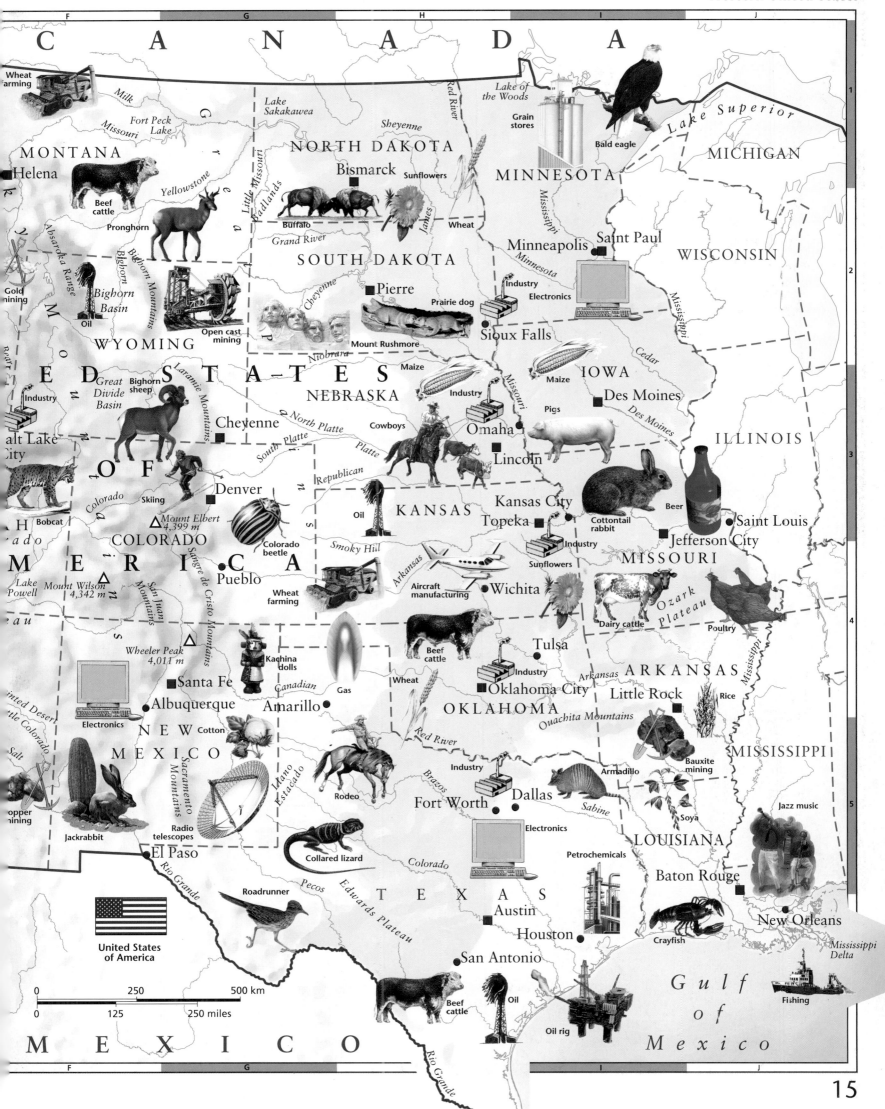

CANADA

Wheat farming

Milk

Fort Peck Lake

Missouri

MONTANA

Helena

Beef cattle

Pronghorn

Yellowstone

Absaroka Range

Bighorn Range

Bighorn Mountains

Gold mining

Bighorn Basin

Oil

Open cast mining

WYOMING

Great Divide Basin

Bighorn sheep

Industry

Laramie Mountains

Salt Lake City

Cheyenne

North Platte

South Platte

Platte

Colorado

Skiing

Denver

Mount Elbert 4,399 m

Republican

Colorado beetle

COLORADO

Sangre de Cristo Mountains

Lake Powell

Mount Wilson 4,342 m

San Juan Mountains

Pueblo

Wheat farming

Smoky Hill

Bobcat

AMERICA

Wheeler Peak 4,011 m

Electronics

Santa Fe

Kachina dolls

Canadian

Gas

Albuquerque

Amarillo

Painted Desert

Little Colorado

Salt

NEW MEXICO

Cotton

Sacramento Mountains

Copper mining

Jackrabbit

Radio telescopes

Llano Estacado

Rodeo

Collared lizard

El Paso

Rio Grande

Roadrunner

Pecos

Edwards Plateau

United States of America

0   250   500 km

0   125   250 miles

TEXAS

Beef cattle

Oil

Oil rig

MEXICO

Rio Grande

NORTH DAKOTA

Lake Sakakawea

Sheyenne

Little Missouri

Badlands

Bismarck

Sunflowers

James

Buffalo

Grand River

SOUTH DAKOTA

Pierre

Prairie dog

Cheyenne

Niobrara

Mount Rushmore

Maize

NEBRASKA

Cowboys

Omaha

Lincoln

KANSAS

Oil

Kansas City

Topeka

Industry

Sunflowers

Aircraft manufacturing

Wichita

Arkansas

Beef cattle

Tulsa

Industry

Wheat

Oklahoma City

OKLAHOMA

Red River

Ouachita Mountains

Industry

Armadillo

Fort Worth

Dallas

Brazos

Sabine

Electronics

Collared lizard

Colorado

Petrochemicals

Austin

Houston

San Antonio

Beef cattle

Crayfish

Red River

Lake of the Woods

Grain stores

Bald eagle

MINNESOTA

Mississippi

Minnesota

Minneapolis

Saint Paul

Industry

Electronics

Sioux Falls

Maize

IOWA

Maize

Des Moines

Pigs

Des Moines

Lincoln

Cottontail rabbit

Beer

Saint Louis

Jefferson City

Industry

MISSOURI

Dairy cattle

Ozark Plateau

Poultry

ARKANSAS

Arkansas

Little Rock

Rice

Bauxite mining

MISSISSIPPI

Soya

Jazz music

LOUISIANA

Baton Rouge

New Orleans

Mississippi Delta

MICHIGAN

Lake Superior

WISCONSIN

Mississippi

Cedar

ILLINOIS

Mississippi

Gulf of Mexico

Fishing

15

Eastern United States

The eastern parts of the USA were home to the first European settlers who arrived in America in the 17th century CE, and they remain the most densely populated areas today. They contain major cities such as New York, Chicago and Washington D.C. Stretching from the rocky shores of Maine down to the sunny islands of Florida Keys, the eastern seaboard (coast) has a varied landscape with many bays and inlets. Further inland, the Appalachian mountain system, which is rich in mineral deposits, cuts through the country. Much of the surrounding area is still covered in trees – in West Virginia, for example, 75 per cent of the land is forest. The states surrounding the Gulf of Mexico enjoy a mostly temperate climate. Florida is warm all year round. It is popular with tourists from the USA and around the world, and is also home to the Kennedy Space Center at Cape Canaveral.

The White House
Situated in Washington D.C. (District of Columbia), the White House is the official home of the President of the United States of America. Washington D.C. is the capital of the USA.

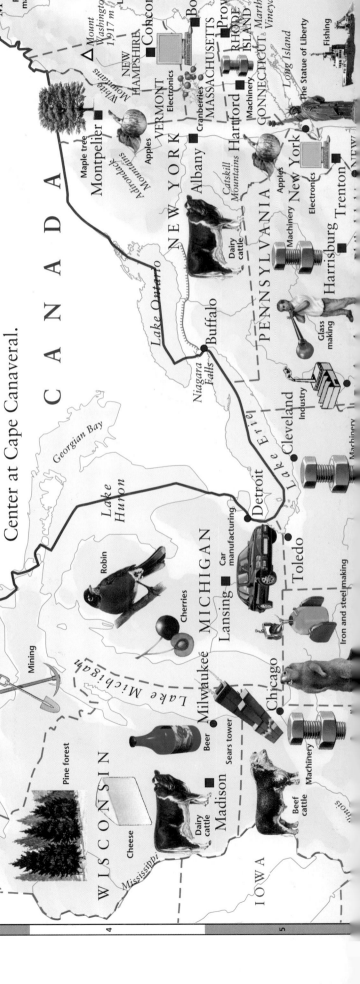

CANADA

MINNESOTA

Lake Superior

Mississippi

Pine forest

Mining

WISCONSIN

Cheese

Dairy cattle

Madison

Beer

Milwaukee

Sears tower

Chicago

Machinery

Beef cattle

IOWA

Lake Michigan

Robin

Cherries

MICHIGAN

Lansing

Car manufacturing

Georgian Bay

Lake Huron

Detroit

Toledo

Iron and steelmaking

Machinery

Lake Erie

Cleveland

Industry

Buffalo

Niagara Falls

Lake Ontario

NEW YORK

Albany

Dairy cattle

Catskill Mountains

Apples

Adirondack Mountains

Maple tree

Montpelier

VERMONT

Apples

Electronics

NEW HAMPSHIRE

Concord

MASSACHUSETTS

Boston

Cape Cod

Nantucket Island

RHODE ISLAND

Providence

CONNECTICUT

Hartford

Machinery

Martha's Vineyard

Long Island

The Statue of Liberty

New York

Electronics

NEW

Trenton

Harrisburg

PENNSYLVANIA

Apples

Machinery

Glass making

MAINE

Augusta

Logging

Paper making

Lobster

Gulf of Maine

Mount Washington 1,917 m

White Mountains

Fishing

Cranberries

Basketball

Basketball is the only major sport to have been invented in the USA. It was invented in 1891ce and involves two teams of five players trying to score by tossing a ball through the opponent's hoop and net, which is called a basket.

FACTS AND FIGURES

Largest cities
New York 18,603,000
Chicago 9,286,000
Philadelphia 5,752,000

Largest lake
Lake Superior 82,350 km²

Highest mountain
Mount Washington 1,917 m

United States
of America

ATLANTIC

OCEAN

BAHAMAS

Gulf

of

Mexico

Gulf Coastal Plain

UNITED STATES

OF

AMERICA

MISSOURI

ILLINOIS
Springfield

INDIANA
Indianapolis

OHIO
Columbus
Cincinnati

KENTUCKY
Frankfort
Louisville

WEST VIRGINIA
Charleston

VIRGINIA
Richmond

WASHINGTON D.C.

MARYLAND
Annapolis
Baltimore

DELAWARE

NEW JERSEY

ARKANSAS

TENNESSEE
Memphis
Nashville
Chattanooga

NORTH CAROLINA
Raleigh
Charlotte

SOUTH CAROLINA
Columbia
Charleston

MISSISSIPPI
Jackson

ALABAMA
Montgomery
Birmingham
Mobile

GEORGIA
Atlanta
Savannah

FLORIDA
Tallahassee
Jacksonville
Orlando
Tampa
Fort Lauderdale
Miami

LOUISIANA

Shellfish
Swordfish
Chesapeake Bay
The White House
Opossum
Tobacco
Eggs
Poultry
Cape Hatteras
Cape Fear
Machinery
Coal mining
Allegheny Mountains
Mount Rogers 1,746 m
Blue Ridge
Appalachian Mountains
Ohio
Wabash
Maize
Soya
Thoroughbred horse
Country music
Cotton
Catfish
Cotton
Cotton
Steamboat
Mississippi Delta
Mississippi
Tennessee
Tombigbee
Alabama
Steel making
Chattahoochee
Raccoon
Skunk
Peaches
Textiles
Tobacco
Savannah
Peanut farming
Cargo ship
Cape San Blas
Epcot Center
Oranges
Cape Canaveral launch site
Cape Canaveral
Brown pelican
Lake Okeechobee
The Everglades
Alligator
Cape Sable
Florida Keys
Tourism

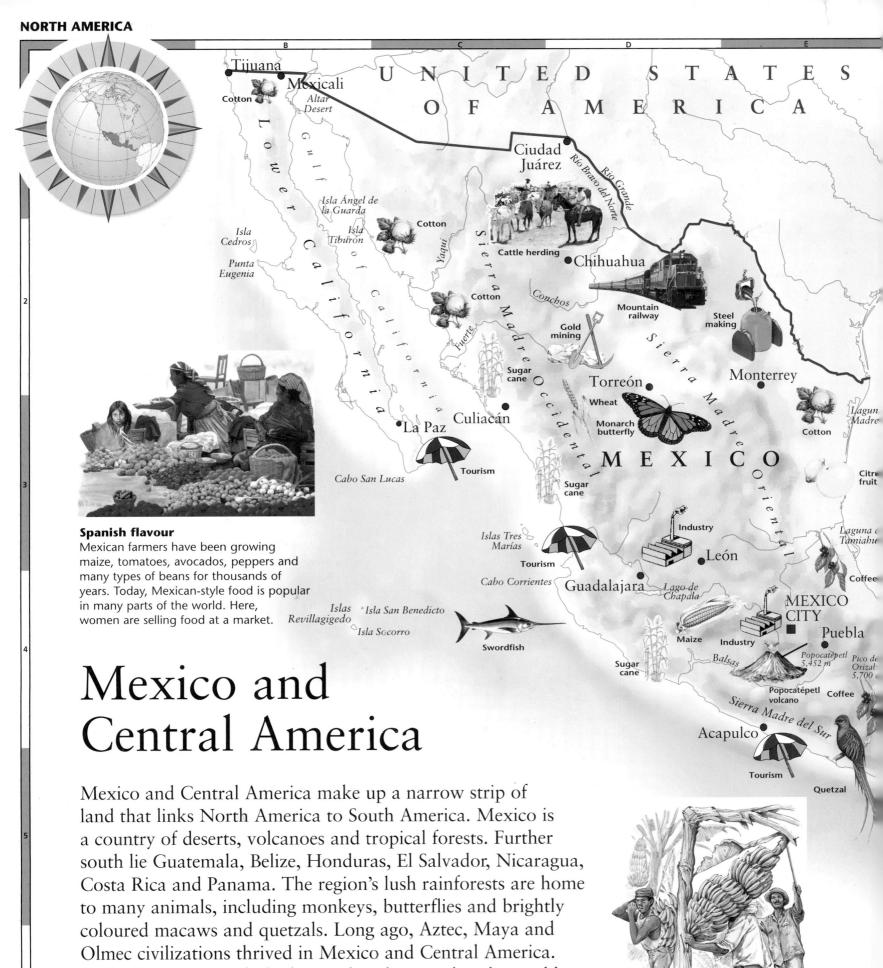

Tijuana
Mexicali
Cotton
Altar Desert

Lower California

Gulf of California

UNITED STATES OF AMERICA

Ciudad Juárez
Río Bravo del Norte
Río Grande

Isla Ángel de la Guarda

Isla Cedros

Isla Tiburón
Yaqui

Punta Eugenia

Cotton

Cattle herding
Chihuahua

Conchos

Mountain railway

Steel making

Fuerte

Cotton

Sierra Madre Occidental

Gold mining

Sugar cane

Torreón
Wheat

Monarch butterfly

Monterrey

Sierra Madre Oriental

Cotton

Lagun Madre

La Paz
Culiacán

Tourism

M E X I C O

Cabo San Lucas

Sugar cane

Citru fruit

Islas Tres Marías

Industry

Laguna Tamiahu

Tourism

León

Cabo Corrientes

Guadalajara

Coffee

Islas Revillagigedo

Isla San Benedicto

Isla Socorro

Swordfish

Lago de Chapala

MEXICO CITY

Puebla

Maize

Industry

Popocatépetl 5,452 m

Pico de Orizaba 5,700

Sugar cane

Balsas

Coffee

Popocatépetl volcano

Sierra Madre del Sur

Acapulco

Tourism

Quetzal

Spanish flavour
Mexican farmers have been growing maize, tomatoes, avocados, peppers and many types of beans for thousands of years. Today, Mexican-style food is popular in many parts of the world. Here, women are selling food at a market.

Mexico and Central America

Mexico and Central America make up a narrow strip of land that links North America to South America. Mexico is a country of deserts, volcanoes and tropical forests. Further south lie Guatemala, Belize, Honduras, El Salvador, Nicaragua, Costa Rica and Panama. The region's lush rainforests are home to many animals, including monkeys, butterflies and brightly coloured macaws and quetzals. Long ago, Aztec, Maya and Olmec civilizations thrived in Mexico and Central America.

The Panama Canal, the busiest big-ship canal in the world, is in Panama. It is 82 km long and links the Pacific and Atlantic oceans. Before it opened in 1914CE, ships had to travel all the way around South America to reach the other ocean.

Going bananas
Bananas are the main crop in Honduras. They account for almost a quarter of the country's income.

Bustling city
Mexico City is the third largest city in the world and home to almost 21 million inhabitants. People enjoy watching bull fighting, or sports such as baseball or football, at these large stadiums.

FACTS AND FIGURES

Largest cities
Mexico City 20,965,000
Guadalajara 3,847,000
Monterrey 3,458,000

Longest river
Rio Grande 3,304 km

Largest lake
Lake Nicaragua, Nicaragua 8,200 km^2

Highest mountain
Pico de Orizaba, Mexico 5,700 m

Gulf of Mexico

Tuna

Lobster

Mexico

Bay of Campeche

Oil rig

Mérida

Chichén Itzá

Yucatan Channel

Isla Cozumel

Yucatan Peninsula

Laguna de Términos

Scarlet macaw

Belize

Istmo de Tehuantepec

Petén

Coffee

Usumacinta

Tikal

Presa de la Angostura

BELIZE

BELMOPAN

Gulf of Honduras

Swan Island (to Honduras)

Honduras

Gulf of Tehuantepec

Sierra Madre

GUATEMALA

Volcán Tajumulco 4,220 m

Coffee

Citrus fruit

Laguna de Caratasca

HONDURAS

Patuca

Coco

Bananas

GUATEMALA CITY

Coffee

Coffee

TEGUCIGALPA

Coffee

Mosquito Coast

SAN SALVADOR

EL SALVADOR

Guatemala

El Salvador

NICARAGUA

Nicaragua

MANAGUA

Lake Nicaragua

San Juan

Panama

COSTA RICA

Douroucouli

Panama Canal

Gulf of Darién

SAN JOSÉ

Mosquito Gulf

PANAMA

PANAMA CITY

Costa Rica

Coffee

Gulf of Panama

COLOMBIA

Gulf of Chiriquí

Isla de Coiba

Keel-billed toucan

0 300 600 km
0 150 300 miles

Temples in the jungle
The Maya people lived in Tikal, Guatemala, over 3,000 years ago. There are more than 3,000 ruined buildings at this site, including impressive temples.

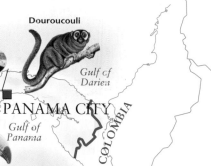

Party time!
Festivals and carnivals are a time to party. People wear colourful costumes and play music as they parade through the streets.

Cuba

Bahamas

Jamaica

Scuba diving

Cigar making

Cruise liner

Fishing

Cutting sugar cane

Tobacco

Sugar cane

Tourism

Mining

Bananas

UNITED STATES OF AMERICA (FLORIDA)

Gulf of Mexico

Tourism

Grand Bahama Island Freeport

Great Abaco

NASSAU
New Providence

Eleuthera Island

Cat Island

B A H A M A S

Andros Island

Long Island

Acklins Island

Straits of Florida

HAVANA

Yucatan Channel

Isla de la Juventud

G

r

e

a

t

e

r

C U B A

Camagüey

Santiago de Cuba

Windw

Cayman Islands (to UK)

Grand Cayman

Montego Bay

JAMAICA

KINGSTON

Navassa Island (to US)

A

The Caribbean

A string of islands separates the Atlantic Ocean from the Caribbean Sea. There are many different countries in the Caribbean and hundreds of islands. Cuba is the largest island, stretching over 1,100 km in length. Haiti and the Dominican Republic share ownership of the second biggest island, Hispaniola. Some of the other islands are so small that no one lives on them. All the islands enjoy a tropical climate with a rainy season between June and November. Occasionally, violent storms, called hurricanes, sweep through the Caribbean. The strong winds and torrential rain can cause serious damage. Coral reefs surround many of the islands, and holidaymakers can scuba dive in the warm waters or explore the islands' many beautiful palm-fringed beaches.

FACTS AND FIGURES

Largest cities
Santo Domingo 2,677,000
Havana 2,198,000
Port-au-Prince 1,557,000

Highest point
Pico Duarte 3,175 m

Number of islands
Over 100

Number of hurricanes
6 per year on average, in the hurricane season between June and November, reaching up to 250 km/h

Beach paradise
Holidaymakers flock to the Caribbean to enjoy the white, sandy beaches. The money they spend there is vital for the countries' economies.

Turks & Caicos Islands (to UK)

Great Inagua

ATLANTIC OCEAN

West Indies

Port-de-Paix

DOMINICAN REPUBLIC

Santiago

Pico Duarte 3,175 m

HAITI

Hispaniola

Cocoa

Mona Passage

Leeward Islands

Puerto Rico (to US)

San Juan

Virgin Islands (to US)

British Virgin Islands (to UK)

Anguilla (to UK)

St Martin (to France & Netherlands)

St Barthélemy (to France)

Barbuda

PORT-AU-PRINCE

SANTO DOMINGO

Netherlands Antilles (to Netherlands)

St Kitts

Nevis

ANTIGUA & BARBUDA

ST JOHN'S

Antigua

Antilles

BASSETERRE

ST KITTS & NEVIS

Montserrat (to UK)

Guadeloupe Passage

Grande Terre

Basse Terre

Guadeloupe (to France)

Haiti

Dominican Republic

St Kitts & Nevis

Antigua & Barbuda

Dominica

DOMINICA **ROSEAU**

Basse Terre

Martinique Passage

Martinique (to France)

Fort-de-France

St Lucia

Caribbean Sea

Shark

Sailing

Lesser Antilles

ST LUCIA

CASTRIES

St Vincent Passage

St Vincent

BARBADOS

BRIDGETOWN

Barbados

KINGSTOWN

ST VINCENT & THE GRENADINES

The Grenadines

Windward Islands

Aruba (to Netherlands)

Oranjestad

Netherlands Antilles (to Netherlands)

Willemstad

Bonaire

Curaçao

COLOMBIA

Grenada

St George's

GRENADA

St Vincent & the Grenadines

Tourism

Tobago

Trinidad & Tobago

PORT-OF-SPAIN

TRINIDAD & TOBAGO

Trinidad

0   250   500 km
0   125   250 miles

V E N E Z U E L A

Aruba
(to Netherlands)
Netherlands Antilles
(to Netherlands)   GRENADA

CARACAS   TRINIDAD & TOBAGO

1

PANAMA

VENEZUELA   GEORGETOWN
PARAMARIBO

GUYANA
■BOGOTÁ   **SURINAM**   Cayenne

COLOMBIA   French
Guiana
(to France)

QUITO

2   **ECUADOR**

B   R   A   Z   I   L

P E R U

LIMA■

3   **B O L I V I A**   BRASÍLIA■

■LA PAZ

■SUCRE

PARAGUAY

4

*Islas de los
Desventurados
(to Chile)*   ASUNCIÓN■

*Juan Fernandez
Islands
(to Chile)*   **URUGUAY**

SANTIAGO■   BUENOS AIRES■   ■MONTEVIDEO

C   **A R G E N T I N A**
H
I
5   L
E

500   1000 km

250   500 miles

6

*Falkland Islands
(to UK)*

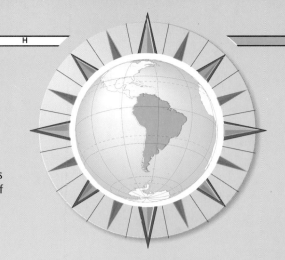

Mighty river
The enormous Amazon river flows across South America and supports a huge variety of life there. These giant lily pads thrive in a section of slow-moving water.

SOUTH AMERICA

South America is the fourth largest continent. It stretches from the Caribbean Sea in the north to the cold lands at its southern tip. In the northeast of the continent lies the tropical Amazon Basin, where it is hot and wet all year round. The mighty Amazon river and Amazon rainforest, the world's largest rainforest, are found there. Further south the climate is cooler and there are great open plains. The longest range of mountains in the world, the Andes, extends for 7,250 km along the western edge of the continent.

Most South American countries are Spanish-speaking, and most of the continent's people live in large cities on the coast.

Rugged mountains
The Torres del Paine National Park is in the far south of Chile. Its unspoilt scenery shows the lakes and mountains at their best.

Haunting music
A young Peruvian girl plays a traditional tune on the rondador or pan-pipes. The notes are made by blowing across the top of hollow bamboo tubes.

Northern South America

The largest tropical rainforest in the world stretches across Northern South America, filling the Amazon Basin. This densely forested region is full of valuable resources, including cacao for chocolate, nuts, rare hardwoods, and plants that can be used to make medicines. But humans are rapidly destroying the rainforests by cutting down the trees for timber and to search for valuable minerals, and clearing the land for agriculture.

Brazil is the largest country in South America and covers almost half of the continent. Much of the world's coffee and sugar cane is grown there. Most of its people live in towns and cities near the coast. Brazil has a very young population – almost half the people are under 20 years old. Venezuela is the richest country in South America as it has huge oil reserves and other minerals. It also has the world's highest waterfall, Angel Falls.

The countries on the western side of the continent are dominated by the Andes Mountains, the longest mountain range in the world. Bolivia has two capitals – La Paz and Sucre. La Paz, the seat of government, high in the Andes, is the world's highest capital city.

Standing tall
The magnificent statue of Christ the Redeemer towers over Rio de Janeiro, Brazil's cultural capital, playground of the rich, and bustling Atlantic port.

Caribbean Sea

Barranquilla
Maracaibo
Gulf of Darien
Lake Maracaibo

PANAMA
Cúcuta
Gulf of Panama

Medellín
Textiles
Oil
Magdalena
Cauca
Llla
Meta

BOGOTÁ
Colombia

Cali
COLOM

Viracocha stone statue
Coff

Fishing
ECUADOR
Bananas

Caquetá

Equator
Ecuador

QUITO
Cotopaxi 5,897 m

Napo
Putumayo

Guayaquil
Chimborazo 6,310 m
Gulf of Guayaquil

Hoatzin
Marañón
Amazon
Ucayali
Juruá

Trujillo

Huascarán 6,768 m
Copper mining

PERU

Machu Picchu

Peru

Callao
LIMA
Cusco
Andes

Nevado Coropuna 6,613 m

Bolivia
Arequipa

PACIFIC
OCEAN

Galapagos Islands
(to Ecuador)
Isla Pinta
Galapagos penguin

0   100 km
0   50 miles

Isla Marchena

Equator

Volcán Wolf 1,646 m
Isla San Salvador

PACIFIC OCEAN

Marine iguana

Isla Fernandina
Santo Tomás 1,490 m

Isla Santa Cruz

Isla San Cristóbal

Isla Isabela

Puerto Baquizero Moreno

Isla Santa María

Giant tortoise
Isla Española

Aruba (to Netherlands)

Netherlands Antilles (to Netherlands)

Valencia

CARACAS

Barquisimeto

Oil

Isla de Margarita

Iron ore mining

Maturín

TRINIDAD & TOBAGO

Guyana

Surinam

Apure

Orinoco

VENEZUELA

Timber

Angel Falls

Cocoa

Guiana Highlands

GEORGETOWN

GUYANA

PARAMARIBO

SURINAM

Cayenne

French Guiana (to France)

Emerald tree boa

Embalse de Gurí

Guaviare

Orinoco

BIA

Negro

Branco

Spider monkey

Esequibo

Scarlet macaw

Mouths of the Amazon

Baía de Marajó

Equator

Amazon

Japurá

Represa de Balbina

Piranha

Amazon

Manaus

Isla de Marajó

Belém

Baía de São Marcos

Basin

Toucan

Amazon

Tapajós

Iriri

Sloth

Represa Tucuruí

Cattle

Industry

Fortaleza

Rainforest

Cabo de São Roque

Coffee

BRAZIL

Purus

Madeira

São Manuel

Xingu

Araguaia

Parnaíba

Sugar cane

Natal

Recife

Brazil nuts

Logging

Tocantins

Bananas

Represa de Sobradinho

Madre de Dios

Beni

Mamoré

Guaporé

Juruena

Cattle

Flanalto de Mato Grosso

Rio das Mortes

Tobacco

Football

São Francisco

Catedral Basílica

Mining

Cocoa

Salvador

BOLIVIA

Nevado de Aneohuma 6,550 m

Paper making

Pantanal

Armadillo

Goiânia

BRASÍLIA

Brazil

LA PAZ

Brazilian

Lake Titicaca

Nevado Sajama 6,542 m

Oruro

SUCRE

Lake Poopó

Tin mining

Altiplano

Maize

Paranaíba

Coffee

Highlands

Belo Horizonte

Citrus fruit

Rio Grande

Industry

Christ the Redeemer

CHILE

PARAGUAY

Paraná

Bananas

São Paulo

Steel making

Rio de Janeiro

ARGENTINA

Serra Geral

Curitiba

ATLANTIC OCEAN

Uruguay

Soya

Porto Alegre

Lagoa dos Patos

Lagoa Mirim

FACTS AND FIGURES

Largest cities
Sao Paulo 17,834,000
Rio de Janeiro 10,872,000

Highest point
Huascarán 6,768 m

Highest waterfall
Angel Falls 978 m

Longest river
Amazon 6,448 km

Largest lake
Lake Titicaca 8,300 km²

0   500   1000 km

0   250   500 miles

Southern South America

Four countries make up Southern South America. They are Chile, Argentina, Paraguay and Uruguay. The Falkland Islands in the Atlantic Ocean are British territories. Chile is a long, thin country sandwiched between the ocean and the high Andes mountains. The driest place in the world, the Atacama desert, is in Chile.

Argentina has a varied landscape, including the jagged peaks of the Andes and the vast flat grasslands of the Pampas region. In the south of the country is Patagonia, a bleak plateau. At the very tip of Southern South America lies the remote and bitterly cold island of Tierra del Fuego, just 1,000 km away from Antarctica.

Uruguay and Argentina share the estuary to the Rio de la Plata, which is a great trading route to the middle of the continent. Paraguay is a landlocked country, which means it has no coasts. Most of the people there are of mixed native American and Spanish descent. In the other countries, many of the people are descendants from European settlers who arrived about 400 years ago.

BRAZIL

PERU

BOLIVIA

PARAGUAY

Paraguay

Hydroelectricity

Soya

Tobacco

Timber

Pantheon of heroes

ASUNCIÓN

Pilcomayo

Gran Chaco

Giant anteater

Tobacco

Ovenbird

Resistencia

Cattle

Posadas

Cotton

Burrowing owl

Santiago del Estero

Salado

Textiles

Laguna Mar Chiquita

Santa Fé

Córdoba

Football

Wine making

San Miguel de Tucumán

Ojos del Salado 6,880 m

Cavy

Rhea

Gaucho

Rosario

Paraná

Uruguay

URUGUAY

Lagoa Mirim

MONTEVIDEO

Río de la Plata

Cattle

Sheep

La Plata

BUENOS AIRES

Mendoza

Wine making

San Rafael

SANTIAGO

Aconcagua 6,960 m

Central Valley

Valparaíso

CHILE

Andean condor

Antofagasta

Atacama Desert

Andes

PACIFIC

Paraguay

Uruguay

26

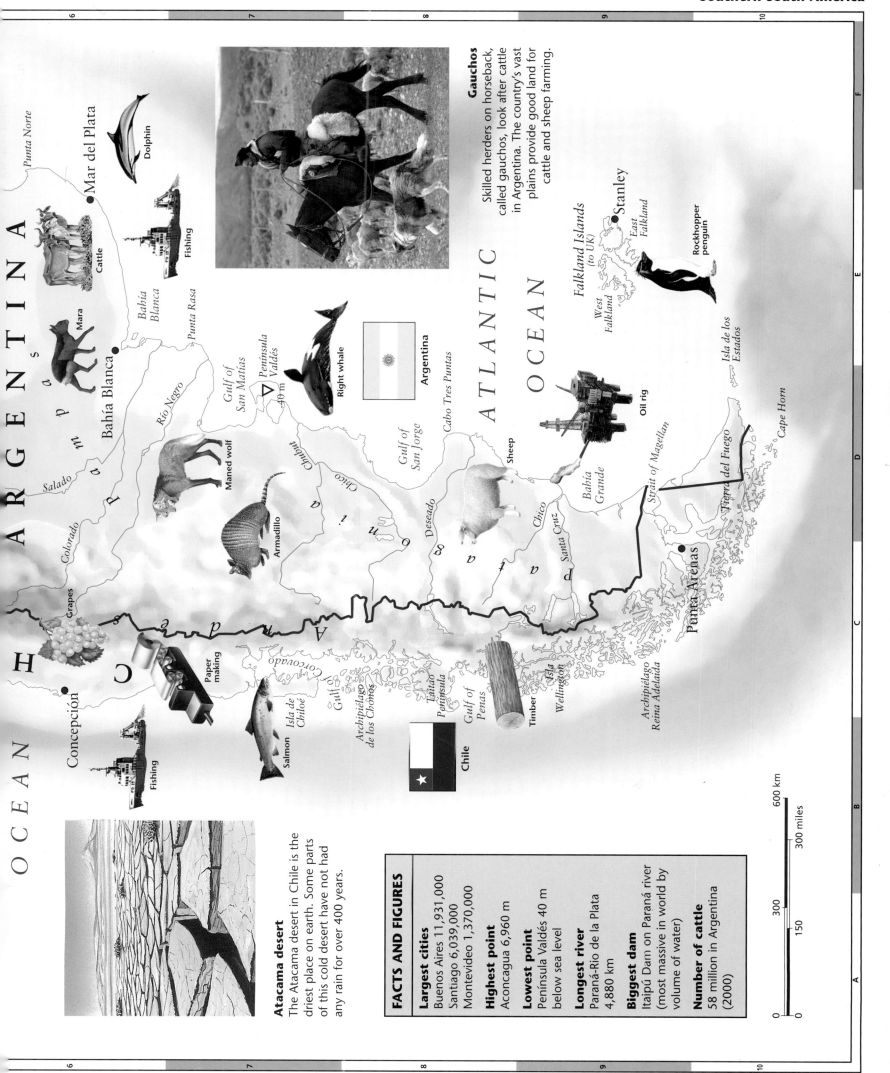

ARGENTINA

Punta Norte

● Mar del Plata

Dolphin

Cattle

Fishing

Bahía Blanca

Punta Rasa

Mara

● Bahía Blanca

Río Negro

Salado

Colorado

Grapes

CHILE

● Concepción

Fishing

Salmon

Paper making

Isla de Chiloé

Gulf of Corcovado

Archipiélago de los Chonos

Taitao Península

Gulf of Penas

Timber

Isla Wellington

Archipiélago Reina Adelaida

● Punta Arenas

Maned wolf

Armadillo

Gulf of San Matías

Península Valdés
40 m

Right whale

Argentina

Chile

Chubut

Chico

Deseado

Gulf of San Jorge

Cabo Tres Puntas

Santa Cruz

Chico

Bahía Grande

Sheep

Oil rig

Strait of Magellan

Tierra del Fuego

Isla de los Estados

Cape Horn

ATLANTIC OCEAN

Falkland Islands (to UK)

● Stanley

West Falkland

East Falkland

Rockhopper penguin

Gauchos

Skilled herders on horseback, called gauchos, look after cattle in Argentina. The country's vast plains provide good land for cattle and sheep farming.

Atacama desert

The Atacama desert in Chile is the driest place on earth. Some parts of this cold desert have not had any rain for over 400 years.

FACTS AND FIGURES

Largest cities
Buenos Aires 11,931,000
Santiago 6,039,000
Montevideo 1,370,000

Highest point
Aconcagua 6,960 m

Lowest point
Península Valdés 40 m
below sea level

Longest river
Paraná-Río de la Plata
4,880 km

Biggest dam
Itaipú Dam on Paraná river
(most massive in world by
volume of water)

Number of cattle
58 million in Argentina
(2000)

600 km
300 miles
300
150
0
0

Greenland
(to Denmark)

0   500   1000 km
0   250   500 miles

Bjørnøya
(to Norway)

Jan Mayen
(to Norway)

REYKJAVIK   ICELAND

Vesterålen
Lofoten

Faeroe Islands
(to Denmark)

Shetland
Islands

N
O
R
W
A
Y

S
W
E
D
E
N

FINLAND

HELSINKI

RUSS

Outer Hebrides

Orkney
Islands

OSLO

STOCKHOLM

Gotland

FEDER

UNITED
KINGDOM

REPUBLIC
OF IRELAND
DUBLIN

Isle of Man
(to UK)

DENMARK

COPENHAGEN

Öland

ESTONIA
TALLINN

RIGA   LATVIA

MOSCOW

LITHUANIA

VILNIUS

NETHERLANDS
AMSTERDAM

BERLIN

RUSS. FED.

MINSK

BELARUS

LONDON

THE HAGUE

WARSAW

Channel Islands
(to UK)

BRUSSELS

BELGIUM

GERMANY

POLAND

KIEV

LUXEMBOURG
PARIS   LUX

PRAGUE

CZECH
REPUBLIC

UKRAINE

FRANCE

VIENNA

SLOVAKIA

BRATISLAVA

BERN   VADUZ   LIECH.
SWITZ   AUSTRIA
LJUBLJANA   SLOVENIA

BUDAPEST
HUNGARY

MOLDOVA
CHISINAU

PORTUGAL

ANDORRA
LA VELLA   ANDORRA

MONACO

ZAGREB
CROATIA

BELGRADE

ROMANIA

BUCHAREST

LISBON
MADRID
SPAIN

SAN
MARINO

BOSNIA &
HERZEGOVINA
SARAJEVO

SERBIA &
MONTENEGRO

BULGARIA

Corsica

ITALY

SOFIA

Mallorca
(Majorca)

Menorca
(Minorca)

ROME
VATICAN
CITY

SKOPJE
MACEDONIA

Eivissa
(Ibiza)

Balearic Islands

Sardinia

TIRANA

Gibraltar
(to UK)

ALBANIA

GREECE

TURKEY

Sicily

MALTA

AFRICA

VALLETTA

Rhodes

ATHENS

Crete

ASIA

IAN

ATION

ASIA

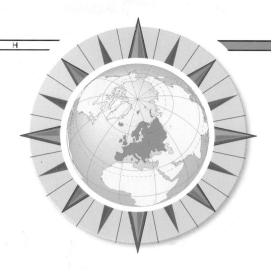

EUROPE

Europe is the second smallest continent, but its 43 countries are heavily populated, making it the most crowded continent of all. It stretches from the lands fringing the Atlantic Ocean in the west to the Ural Mountains in the Russian Federation in the east, and from the Baltic Sea in the north to the Mediterranean Sea in the south. It is a continent of peninsulas and islands and its ragged coastline measures almost 61,000 km. If stretched out, this would circle the Equator just over one-and-a-half times. Much of Europe is mountainous. The countries around the Mediterranean enjoy hot, dry summers and warm, wet winters. The climate in much of the rest of Europe is quite mild.

Many of the countries in Europe have existed for hundreds of years; others have been formed very recently and are just a few years old.

National traditions
Many countries have strong traditions. These girls are dressed in the national costume of Latvia.

Rugged coastline
The Balearic Islands, shown here, are just some of the many islands and coastal regions throughout Europe that are enjoyed by visitors every year.

Northwestern Europe

Four countries in northwestern Europe make up the area called Scandinavia: Norway, Sweden, Finland and Denmark. Far to the west of these lies the volcanic island of Iceland. The far north of Scandinavia is deep inside the Arctic Circle, but its cold climate is tempered by the North Atlantic Drift, an ocean current that carries warm water across the Atlantic Ocean.

The Scandinavian landscape is rugged, mountainous and wooded. Along the coast of Norway are long, deep sea inlets called fjords. There are also thousands of lakes – Sweden alone has over 95,000. Norway has five of the world's highest waterfalls – Utigard, Mongefossen, Espelandsfoss, Ostre Mardola Foss and Tyssestrengane. Over half of Sweden's land surface is covered with dense forest. Denmark's land, by contrast, is mainly flat, and much of it is used for farmland.

Iceland is partly covered by ice fields and glaciers. The land is volcanic and has many geysers and hot springs.

FACTS AND FIGURES

Largest cities
Stockholm 1,661,000
Copenhagen 1,386,000

Largest lake
Lake Vänern 5,585 km²

Highest point
Galdhøpiggen 2,479 m

Highest waterfall
Utigard (800 m) is the third highest in the world

Iceland

Iceland

ICELAND

REYKJAVÍK

Keflavík

Faxaflói

Breidhafjördhur

Arctic Circle

Húnaflói

Akureyi

Geyser

Vatnajökull

△ Hvannadalshnúkur 2,119 m

Cod

Puffin

ATLANTIC OCEAN

200 km
100 miles

100
50
0

Main map

RUSSIAN FEDERATION

Barents Sea

Varangerfjorden

Kirkenes

Lemming

Tana

Teno joki

Porsangen

North Cape

Magerøya

Seiland

Reindeer

Rolvsøya

Sørøya

Inarijärvi

Lokan Tekojärvi

Oulu

Kemijoki

Kemi

Luleå

Ounasjoki

Tornionjoki

Kalixälven

Lapland

Sami people

Iron ore mining

Steel making

Muonioälven

Torneträsk

△ Kebnekaise 2,111 m

Kiruna

Luleälven

Skellefteälven

Fish processing

Tromsø

Ringvassøy

Kvaløya

Senja

Narvik

Pine marten

Logging

Rødvathet

Storgjellet

Andøya

Langøya

Hinnøya

Austvågøy

Vestvågøy

Vestfjorden

Bodø

Suanisen

Lofoten

Moskenesøy

Cod

Norwegian Sea

Fjords

Vega

Vikna

Fishing

ARCTIC OCEAN

Norway

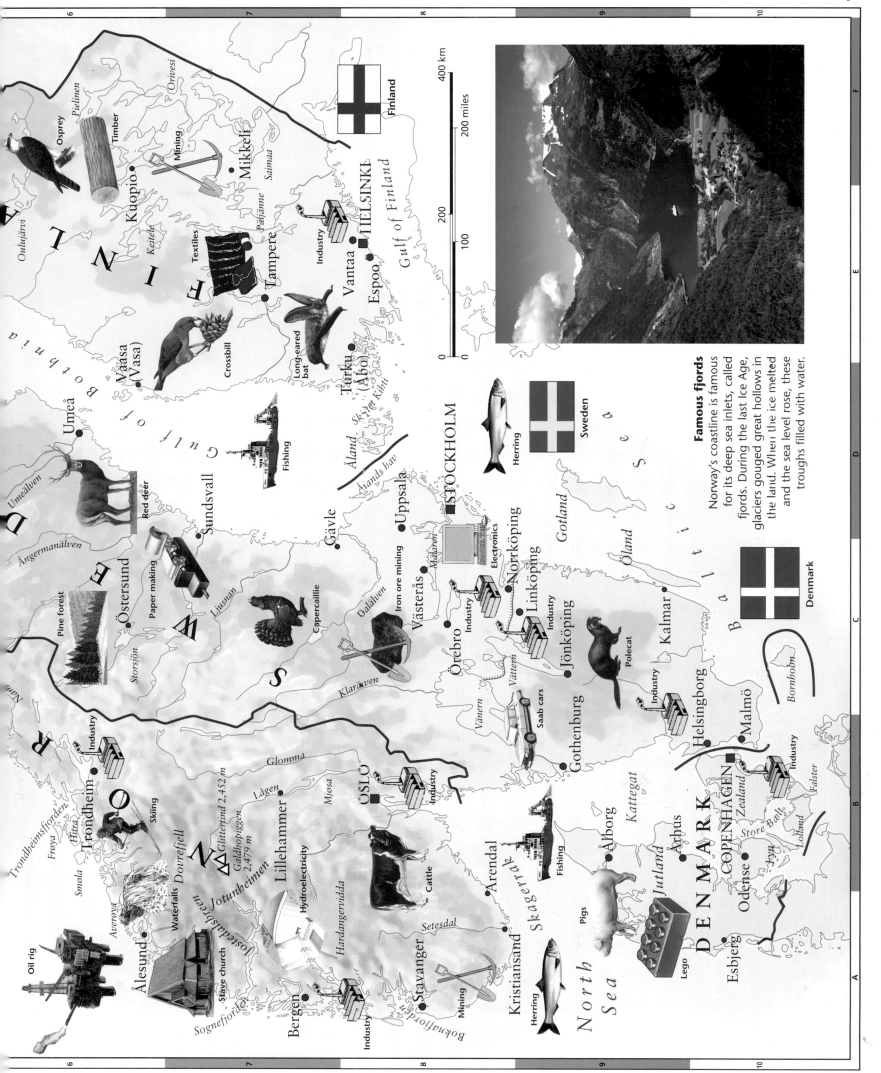

Famous fjords

Norway's coastline is famous for its deep sea inlets, called fjords. During the last Ice Age, glaciers gouged great hollows in the land. When the ice melted and the sea level rose, these troughs filled with water.

Finland

Sweden

Denmark

Osprey

Timber

Mining

Kuopio

Mikkeli

Pielinen

Orivesi

Oulujärvi

Keitele

Saimaa

Päijänne

Textiles

Tampere

Industry

Vantaa

Espoo

HELSINKI

Gulf of Finland

F I N L A N D

Vaasa (Vasa)

Crossbill

Long-eared bat

Turku (Åbo)

Skärgät Kihti

Åland

Åbands hav

Umeå

Umeälven

Red deer

Sundsvall

Fishing

Gävle

Uppsala

STOCKHOLM

Herring

Gotland

Öland

B a l t i c   S e a

Ångermanälven

Östersund

Paper making

Pine forest

Storsjön

Liusnan

Capercaillie

Oalälven

Iron ore mining

Västerås

Mälaren

Electronics

Norrköping

Linköping

Industry

Jönköping

Kalmar

Bornholm

Nam

J Ä M

S V E R I G E

Klarälven

Örebro

Vättern

Saab cars

Gothenburg

Industry

Polecat

Helsingborg

Malmö

Vänern

Glomma

Industry

Trondheimsfjorden

Trondheim

Hitra

Smola

Froya

Averoya

Oil rig

Ålesund

Waterfalls

Dovrefjell

Jostedalsbreen

Skiing

Glittertind 2.452 m

Galdhopiggen 2.479 m

Jotunheimen

Lillehammer

Lågen

Mjosa

OSLO

Industry

Hardangervidda

Hydroelectricity

Cattle

Setesdal

Stave church

Bergen

Sognefjorden

Mining

Industry

Boknafjorden

Stavanger

Kristiansand

Herring

Arendal

Skagerrak

N O R G E

North Sea

Pigs

Fishing

Ålborg

Kattegat

Århus

Jutland

Esbjerg

Odense

Fyn

Store Bælt

Zealand

Lolland

COPENHAGEN

Industry

Falster

D E N M A R K

Lego

400 km

200 miles

200

100

0

The British Isles

The British Isles are made up of two large islands and many smaller ones that lie off the coast of northwest Europe, surrounded by the Atlantic Ocean. The two larger islands are Great Britain and Ireland. Great Britain consists of England, Scotland and Wales, which together with the northern part of Ireland, called Northern Ireland, make up the United Kingdom. The rest of Ireland, the Republic of Ireland, is a separate country.

The British Isles enjoy a mild climate, which is influenced by the warm Gulf Stream. This is an ocean current that carries warm water from the Straits of Florida across the Atlantic towards western Europe, helping to keep the area warm. Winters can be snowy and wet, with cold winds coming from the north or east. Summers are generally warm, although winds from the southwest do bring rain.

Much of the land is used for farming. But nearly 90 per cent of the population live in towns and cities. In the 19th century CE, many factories were built and big cities grew to support them. Today, the factories have declined, and more people work in service industries, such as banking and insurance.

London's skyline
The dome of St Paul's Cathedral stands high above the surrounding buildings. Built by Sir Christopher Wren in CE1672, the dome is one of the finest in the world.

FACTS AND FIGURES

Largest cities
London 8,201,000
Birmingham 2,373,000
Manchester 2,353,000
Glasgow 1,168,000
In CE1900, London was the biggest city in the world

Largest lake
Lough Neagh 396 km²

Longest lake
Loch Ness 35 km

Longest river
Shannon 372 km

Highest mountain
Ben Nevis 1,343 m

Total number of islands
Over 5,000

Lerwick

Fair Isle

Shetland Islands

Mainland

Fishing

Grey seal

Seagull

Cod

Orkney Islands

Mainland

Kirkwall

Hoy

Wick

Oil rig

Aberdeen

Red deer

Dee

Don

Ben Macdhui 1,309 m

Dundee

Perth

Edinburgh castle

Firth of Forth

S C O T L A N D

Spey

Moray Firth

Inverness

Loch Ness

Grampian Mountains

Ben Nevis 1,343 m

Skiing

Northwest Highlands

Fort William

Loch Lomond

Oban

Cape Wrath

Sheep

Puffin

The Minch

Mull

Jura

Colonsay

Lewis

Harris

Skye

The Little Minch

Eigg

Rhum

Muck

Coll

Tiree

Canna

Inner Hebrides

H e b r i d e s

O u t e r

North Uist

South Uist

Benbecula

Barra

Saint Kilda

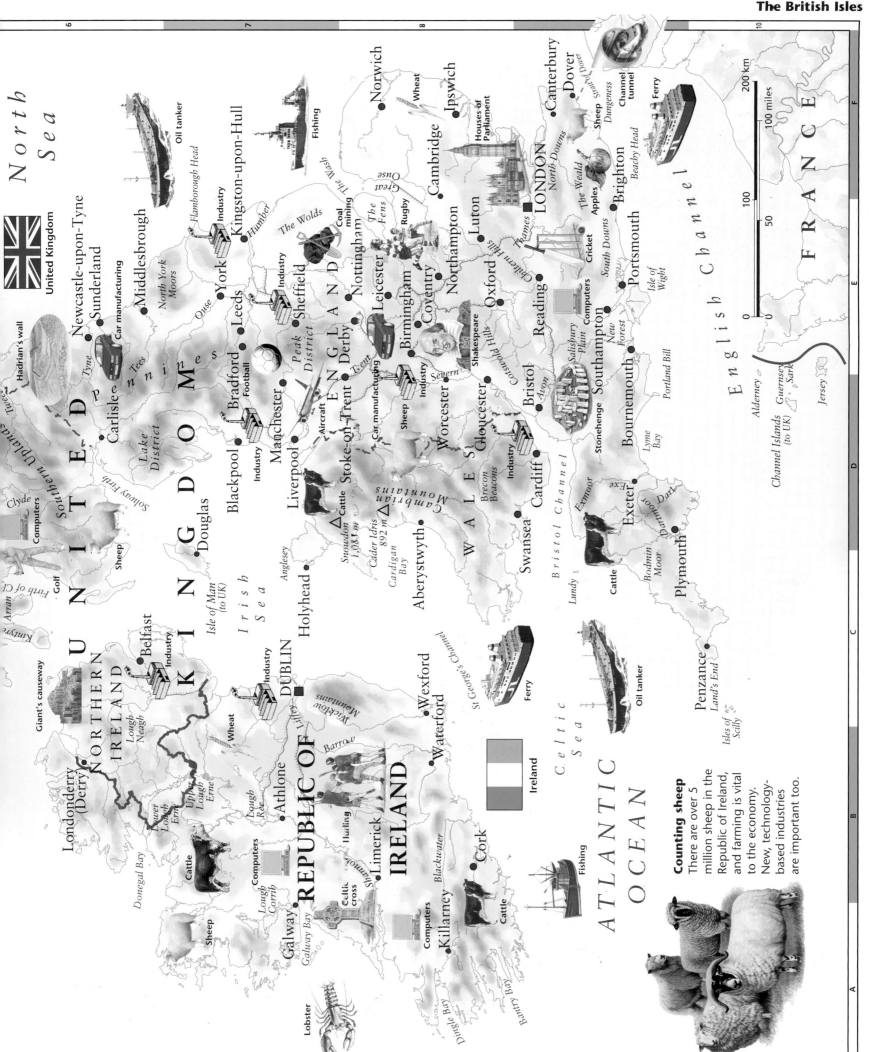

Counting sheep
There are over 5 million sheep in the Republic of Ireland, and farming is vital to the economy. New, technology-based industries are important too.

Germany and the Low Countries

Belgium, the Netherlands and Luxembourg are small countries where the land is low and flat. Because of this, they are also known as the Low Countries. About 40 per cent of the land in the Netherlands has been reclaimed from the sea. To hold back the water, dykes or sea walls have been built. The reclaimed land is excellent farming land and the Netherlands is known for its agricultural goods, especially dairy products and flowers. Belgium, too, is mostly flat, and also relies on dykes to hold back the sea. Much of tiny Luxembourg is rolling plateau land, and fertile farmland is found here.

Germany is a large country – the fourth largest in Europe. The central area is made up of highlands and plateaux. The Bohemian Forest is found further south. Further south still are the Bavarian Alps, which border Austria. The Black Forest, in the southwest of the country, is mountainous and popular with tourists.

All four countries are prosperous and their people enjoy a high standard of living. Belgium's capital, Brussels, contains the major offices of the European Union. Luxembourg is an important banking centre. Germany was divided into two countries, East Germany and West Germany, for 45 years before it became one country again in 1990. It is now Europe's leading industrial country.

Living in the cold

The climate in the higher areas of the Black Forest, in Germany, is raw and cold in winter, but the valleys are mild and have good pasture lands. Winter sports are popular here. The distinctive houses are built with steeply sloping roofs so that any snow will slide off them.

FACTS AND FIGURES

Largest cities
Berlin 4,064,000
Amsterdam 1,121,000
Brussels 1,076,000

Highest mountain
Zugspitze 2,963 m

Longest river
Danube 2,858 km

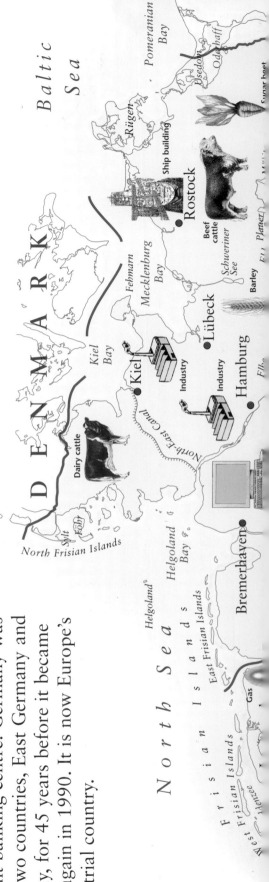

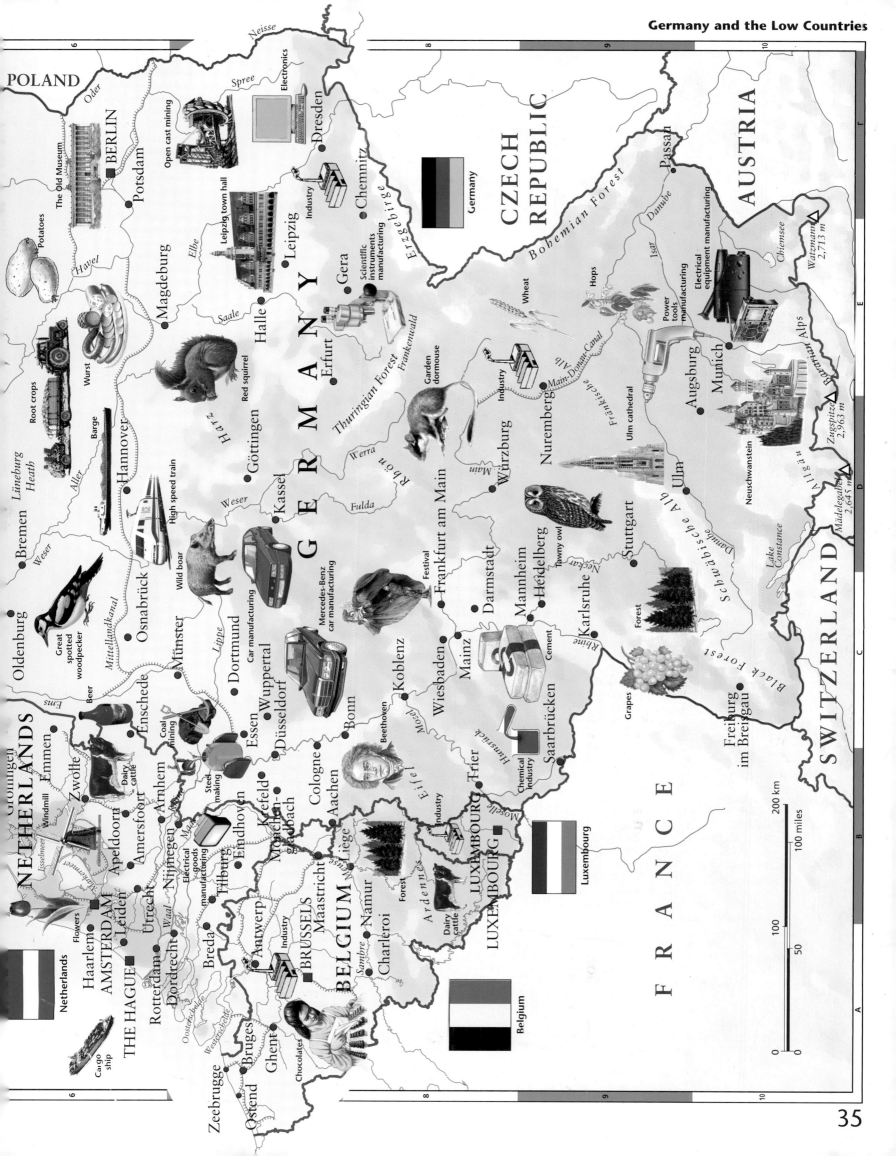

POLAND

Oder
Neisse
Spree
Electronics
BERLIN
The Old Museum
Potsdam
Open cast mining
Dresden
Chemnitz
Erzgebirge
Industry
Leipzig
Leipzig town hall
Elbe
Gera
Scientific instruments manufacturing
Potatoes
Havel
Magdeburg
Saale
Halle
Erfurt
Thuringian Forest
Frankenwald
Wurst
Root crops
Barge
Hannover
Red squirrel
Harz
Göttingen
Kassel
Weser
Werra
Fulda
Rhön
Bremen
Lüneburg Heath
Weser
Aller
High speed train
Mittellandkanal
Osnabrück
Great spotted woodpecker
Oldenburg
Ems
Münster
Lippe
Wild boar
Dortmund
Car manufacturing
Mercedes-Benz car manufacturing
Wuppertal
Essen
Düsseldorf
Beer
Coal mining
Enschede
Steel making
Arnhem
Dairy cattle
Zwolle
Emmen
Groningen
Windmill
IJsselmeer
Haarlem
AMSTERDAM
Leiden
Utrecht
THE HAGUE
Rotterdam
Dordrecht
Breda
Waal
Maas
Nijmegen
Amersfoort
Apeldoorn
Electrical goods manufacturing
Eindhoven
Tilburg
Krefeld
Mönchengladbach
Aachen
Cologne
Bonn
Koblenz
Mosel
Eifel
Trier
Moselle
Hunsrück
Chemical industry
Saarbrücken
Cement
Rhine
Wiesbaden
Mainz
Darmstadt
Mannheim
Heidelberg
Karlsruhe
Neckar
Tawny owl
Stuttgart
Forest
Freiburg im Breisgau
Grapes
Black Forest
Schwäbische Alb
Frankfurt am Main
Festival
Beethoven
Würzburg
Main
Nuremberg
Main-Donau-Canal
Fränkische Alb
Ulm
Ulm cathedral
Danube
Schwäbische Alb
Allgäu
Neuschwanstein
Bavarian Alps
Augsburg
Munich
Isar
Danube
Passau
Hops
Wheat
Industry
Garden dormouse
Power tools manufacturing
Electrical equipment manufacturing
AUSTRIA
CZECH REPUBLIC
Bohemian Forest
Chiemsee
Watzmann 2,713 m
Zugspitze 2,963 m
Mädelegabel 2,645 m
Lake Constance
SWITZERLAND

GERMANY

Germany

NETHERLANDS
Flowers
Cargo ship
Zeebrugge
Ostend
Oosterschelde
Westerschelde
Bruges
Ghent
Chocolates
Antwerp
Industry
BRUSSELS
BELGIUM
Namur
Charleroi
Sambre
Maastricht
Liège
Meuse
Ardennes
Forest
Dairy cattle
LUXEMBOURG
LUXEMBOURG

Netherlands

Belgium

Luxembourg

FRANCE

200 km
100 miles
100
50
0
0

France

France is the largest country in western Europe. The land changes greatly across the country. In the northeast the Vosges Mountains form a border with Germany, while the Alps separate France from Italy. The southwestern border is formed by the Pyrenees, and to the west is the Atlantic Ocean. There are rugged highlands in central France, and also many beautiful river valleys. Corsica, the fourth largest island in the Mediterranean, belongs to France.

The climate varies across such a large area, which means that many different crops can be grown. These include wheat, maize, peaches and grapes, which are made into some of the world's finest wines. French food is also of high quality and French cooking is enjoyed all over the world.

Tourism plays a large part in the French economy. Every year, thousands of people enjoy holidays along the warm Mediterranean coast, in the French countryside or in the cold, snowy mountainous regions, where winter sports such as skiing are popular.

The tiny nation of Monaco, on the south coast near the Italian border, is the second smallest independent country in the world.

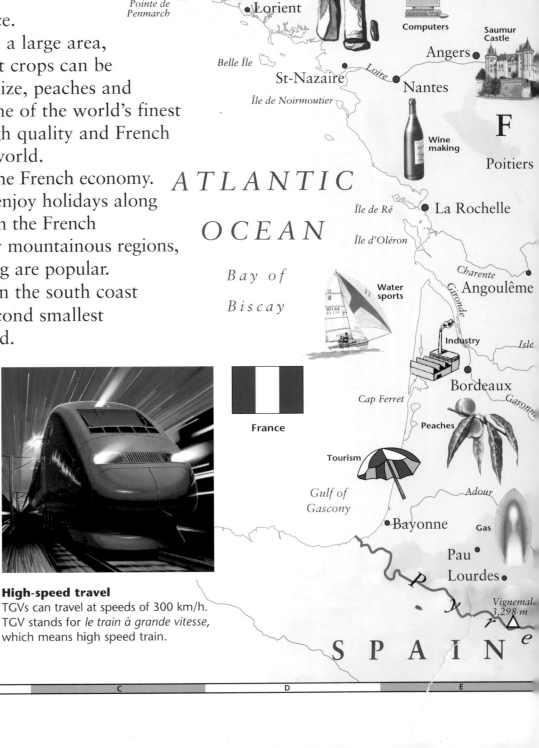

FACTS AND FIGURES

Largest cities
Paris 9,645,000
Marseille 1,350,000
Lyon 1,349,000

Longest river
Loire 1,020 km

Highest mountain
Mont Blanc 4,810 m. This is the second highest mountain in Europe

Number of tourists
75 million visitors per year (2000)

High-speed travel
TGVs can travel at speeds of 300 km/h. TGV stands for *le train à grande vitesse*, which means high speed train.

GERMANY

BELGIUM

LUXEMBOURG

Strait of Dover

Dunkerque
Calais
Boulogne-sur-Mer
Lille
Lens
Arras

Channel tunnel

Dieppe
Amiens
Somme
Oise

Rouen
Seine

Eiffel tower

Versailles
PARIS
Cars

Chartres cathedral
Chartres

Orléans
Hoopoe
Tours
Cher

Bourges
Morvan
Loire

R A N C E

Creuse

Tour de France

Vienne

Clermont-Ferrand
Limoges

Puy de Sancy △ 1,885 m

TGV

St-Étienne

Lascaux cave paintings

Massif

Dordogne

Lot

Wine making

Sunflowers

Aircraft manufacturing

Tarn

Central

Cévennes

Toulouse
Maize

Canal du Midi

Brown bear
Carcassonne

Skiing
Wine making
Perpignan

Olives

ANDORRA

e s

Reims

Grapes

Wheat
Seine
Yonne

Troyes

Wild boar

Wine making

Dijon

Thionville
Metz

Nancy
Strasbourg

Mulhouse

Meuse
Marne
Moselle
Wheat

Vosges

Iron ore mining

Coal mining
Wine making

Besançon

Wine making

Saône

Jura

SWITZERLAND

LIECHTENSTEIN

AUSTRIA

A l p s

Lake Geneva

Chamonix △
Mont Blanc 4,810 m

ITALY

Lyon
Annecy

Industry

Coal mining

Grenoble

Isère

Les Écrins △ 4,102 m

Skiing

Valence

Chamois

Rhône

Orange
Avignon

Nîmes

Durance

Maritime Alps

Perfume

Aix-en-Provence

Industry

Marseille

Toulon

MONACO
MONACO
Nice
Cannes
Tourism

Côte d'Azur
Îles d'Hyères

Montpellier
Camargue
Flamingoes

Gulf of Lion

Mediterranean Sea

Monaco

Fine wines
Vineyards of grapes grow throughout much of France, to be made into wines and spirits.

0   100   200 km
0   50   100 miles

Cap Corse
Bastia
Tourism

Corsica

Ajaccio

Sartène
Bonifacio
Strait of Bonifacio

Spain and Portugal

The countries of Spain, Portugal and tiny Andorra make up the Iberian Peninsula, a land mass that juts out from southern Europe. It has a varied landscape, with mountains called sierras and a broad central plateau. The lands along the northern and western coasts are fertile farming regions and benefit from Atlantic rains. Madrid, in the heart of Spain, bakes under the hot summer sun, but has cold winters. It is the capital of Spain, and is a lively and bustling city, where the people love to party.

Further south on the Mediterranean coast, the climate is hotter, making the region popular with tourists. The climate along the coasts of Portugal is cooler, with warm summers and milder winters.

Andorra is a tiny country high in the Pyrenees. Winters there can be harsh, with lots of snow, but summers are sunny and dry.

Gibraltar is a tiny British colony, linked to Spain by a narrow strip of land only 3 km long.

FACTS AND FIGURES

Largest cities
Madrid 5,087,000
Barcelona 3,300,000
Lisbon 2,900,000

Longest river
Tagus 1,007 km

Highest mountain
Mulhacén 3,478 m

Highest capital
Andorra La Vella is the highest capital city in Europe

Bay of Biscay

A Coruña

Santiago de Compostela

Gijón

Oviedo

Costa

Brown bear

Cordillera Cantábrica

León

Vigo

Miño

Ourense

Potatoes

Mining

Wheat

Embalse de Ricobayo

Valladolid

Wine making

Porto

Douro

Mining

Grapes

Potatoes

Embalse de Almendra

Salamanca

Portugal

Coimbra

Serra da Estrela

PORTUGAL

S i s t

Tagus

S

P

Embalse de Alcántara

Embalse de Valdecañas

Cáceres

Embalse de Cijara

Santarém

Industry

Tagus

LISBON

Cork trees

Badajoz

Sheep

Setúbal

Cabo Espichel

Alqueva Reservoir

Great Mosque at Cordoba

A l e n t e j o

Guadiana

S i e r r a   M o r e n a

Córdoba

Sardines

Iberian lynx

Guadalquivir

Seville

Flamenco dancers

Tourism

A l g a r v e

Citrus fruit

Huelva

Dos Hermanas

Lagos

Cabo de São Vicente

Tavira

Faro

Gulf of Cádiz

Jerez de la Frontera

Wine making

Barbary ape

S i s

Fishing

Tuna

Cádiz

Costa de la Luz

Marbella

ATLANTIC OCEAN

Gibraltar (to UK)

Strait of Gibraltar

Ceuta (to Spain)

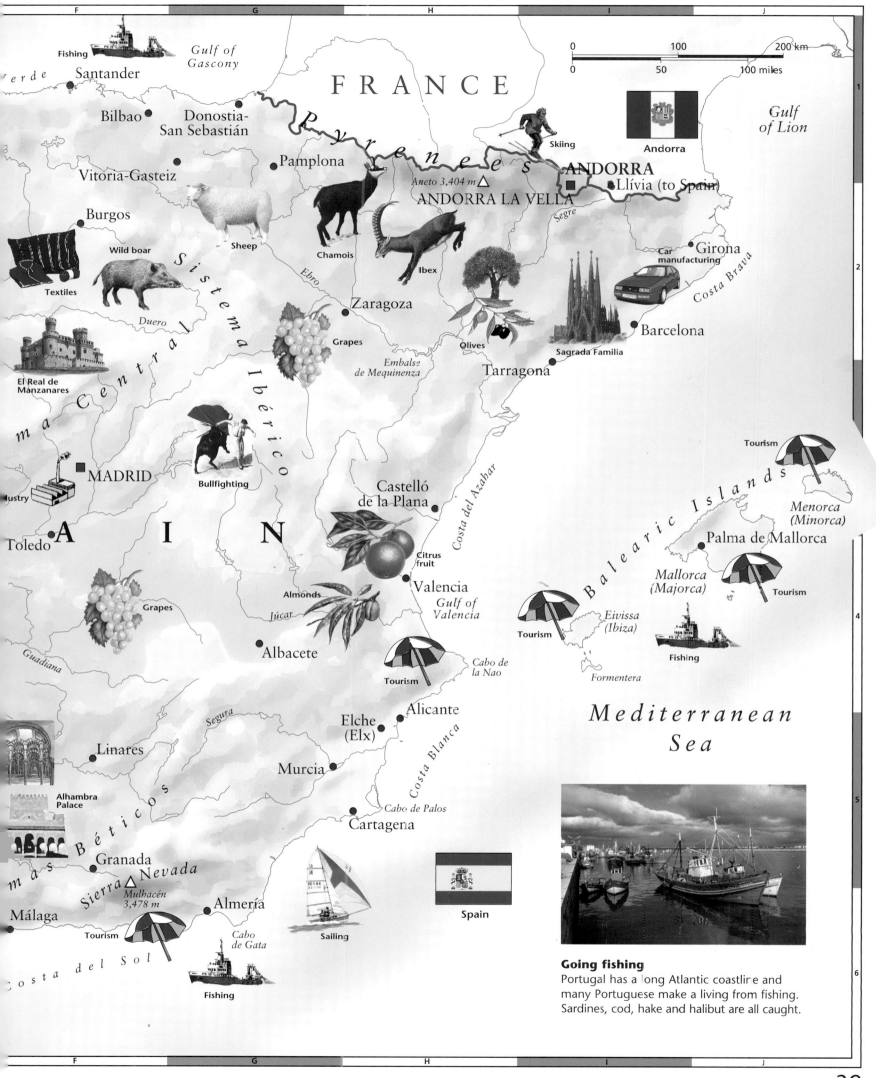

Fishing

Gulf of Gascony

Santander

Bilbao

Donostia-
San Sebastián

F R A N C E

0   100   200 km

0   50   100 miles

*Gulf
of Lion*

Skiing

Andorra

Vitoria-Gasteiz

Pamplona

P y r e n e e s

Aneto 3,404 m △

ANDORRA

Llívia (to Spain)

Burgos

Sheep

Chamois

ANDORRA LA VELLA

Segre

Car
manufacturing

Girona

Wild boar

*S
i
s
t
e
m
a
C
e
n
t
r
a
l*

Ibex

Costa Brava

Textiles

Duero

*S
i
s
t
e
m
a
I
b
é
r
i
c
o*

Grapes

Zaragoza

*Embalse
de Mequinenza*

Olives

Sagrada Familia

Barcelona

El Real de
Manzanares

Tarragona

Bullfighting

MADRID

Ebro

Tourism

dustry

*B a l e a r i c
I s l a n d s*

A

I

N

Castelló
de la Plana

Costa del Azahar

*Menorca
(Minorca)*

Toledo

Palma de Mallorca

Citrus
fruit

*Mallorca
(Majorca)*

Tourism

Grapes

Almonds

Júcar

Valencia

*Gulf of
Valencia*

*Eivissa
(Ibiza)*

Tourism

Guadiana

Albacete

Tourism

Fishing

*Cabo de
la Nao*

Formentera

Segura

Tourism

Alicante

M e d i t e r r a n e a n

Linares

Elche
(Elx)

Costa Blanca

S e a

Alhambra
Palace

Murcia

Cabo de Palos

*m a s
B é t i c o s*

Cartagena

Granada

Sierra Nevada

Mulhacén
3,478 m △

Almería

Sailing

Spain

Málaga

Tourism

*Cabo
de Gata*

Costa del Sol

Fishing

Going fishing
Portugal has a long Atlantic coastline and
many Portuguese make a living from fishing.
Sardines, cod, hake and halibut are all caught.

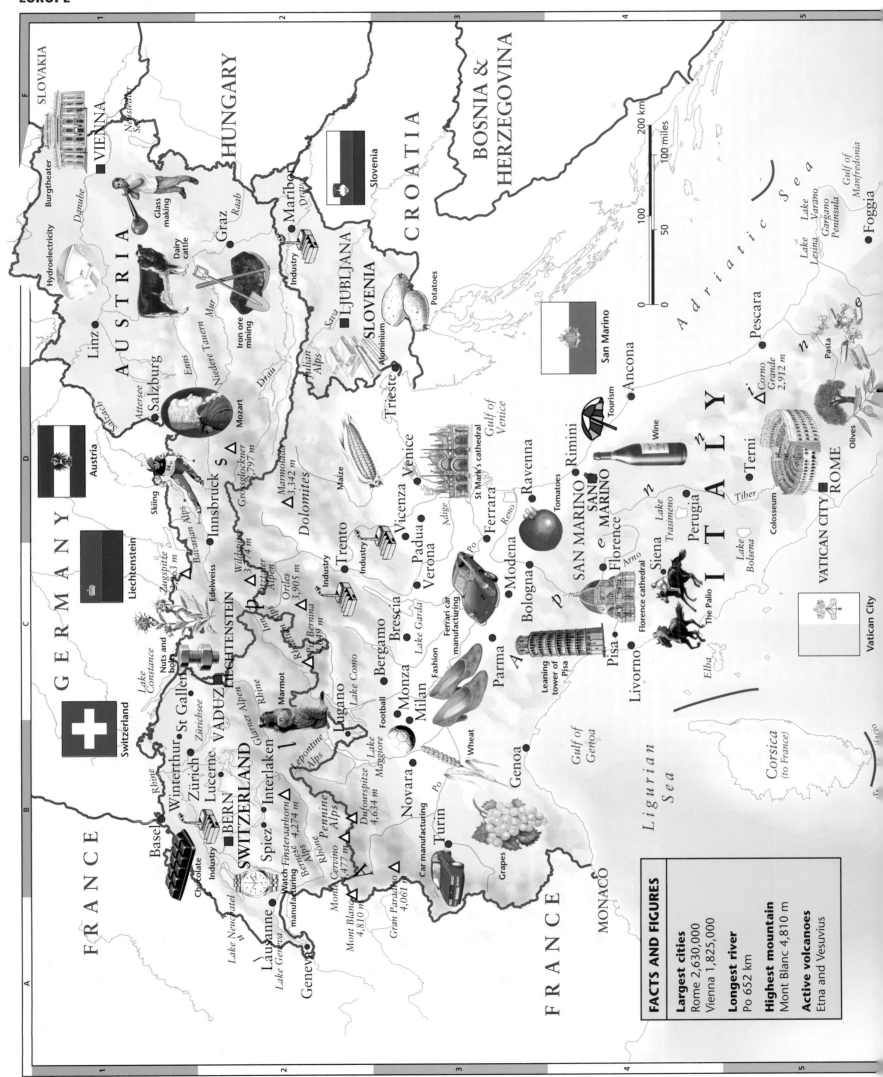

SLOVAKIA

VIENNA ■

Burgtheater

Neusiedler See

Hydroelectricity

Danube

Glass making

HUNGARY

Dairy cattle

Graz

Raab

Linz ●

A U S T R I A

Salzburg ●

Mozart

Attersee

Niedere Tauern

Enns

Salzach

Mur

Iron ore mining

Maribor ●

Drava

Industry

Slovenia

LJUBLJANA ■

SLOVENIA

Sava

Potatoes

Aluminium

Drau

Julian Alps

Trieste

C R O A T I A

BOSNIA & HERZEGOVINA

Adriatic Sea

Gulf of Manfredonia

Foggia ●

Lake Varano

Gargano Peninsula

Lake Lesina

Skiing

Bavarian Alps

Innsbruck ●

Grossglockner 3,797 m

Marmolada 3,342 m

△ Dolomites

Maize

Vicenza

Venice ●

St Mark's cathedral

Gulf of Venice

Tourism

Ancona ●

San Marino

Pescara ●

△ Corno Grande 2,912 m

n e

Pasta

G E R M A N Y

Austria

Liechtenstein

Zugspitze 2,963 m

Wildspitze 3,774 m

Edelweiss

Ötztaler Alpen

Ortles 3,905 m

Trento ●

Industry

Padua ●

Verona ●

Adige

Ferrara ●

Ravenna ●

Reno

Tomatoes

SAN MARINO

Rimini ●

Wine

I T A L Y

Terni ●

Tiber

Olives

Switzerland

Lake Constance

St Gallen

Winterthur ●

Zürich ●

Zürichsee

LIECHTENSTEIN

VADUZ ■

Rhine

Glarner Alpen

Rhine

Piz Bernina 4,049 m

Industry

Bergamo ●

Brescia ●

Lake Garda

Fashion

Ferrari car manufacturing

Modena ●

Bologna ●

San Marino

Florence ●

Arno

Florence cathedral

SAN MARINO

Perugia ●

Siena ●

The Palio

Lake Trasimeno

Lake Bolsena

Colosseum

VATICAN CITY ■

ROME ■

Vatican City

Nuts and bolts

Marmot

Lugano ●

Lake Como

Lake Maggiore

Lepontine Alps

Monza ●

Milan ●

Pisa ●

Leaning tower of Pisa

Livorno ●

Parma ●

A p

Elba

Basel ●

Winterthur

Zürich

Lucerne ●

Rhine

Chocolate

Industry

SWITZERLAND

BERN ■

Spiez ●

Interlaken ●

Finsteraarhorn 4,274 m

Bernese Alps

Football

Wheat

Genoa ●

Gulf of Genoa

Ligurian Sea

Corsica (to France)

Lausanne ●

Lake Neuchâtel

Watch manufacturing

Monte Cervino 4,477 m

Rhône

Pennine Alps

Dufourspitze 4,634 m

Novara ●

Car manufacturing

Turin ●

Po

Grapes

Geneva ●

Lake Geneva

Mont Blanc 4,810 m

Gran Paradiso 4,061 m

F R A N C E

MONACO

FACTS AND FIGURES

Largest cities
Rome 2,630,000
Vienna 1,825,000

Longest river
Po 652 km

Highest mountain
Mont Blanc 4,810 m

Active volcanoes
Etna and Vesuvius

200 km

100 miles

100

50

0   0

40

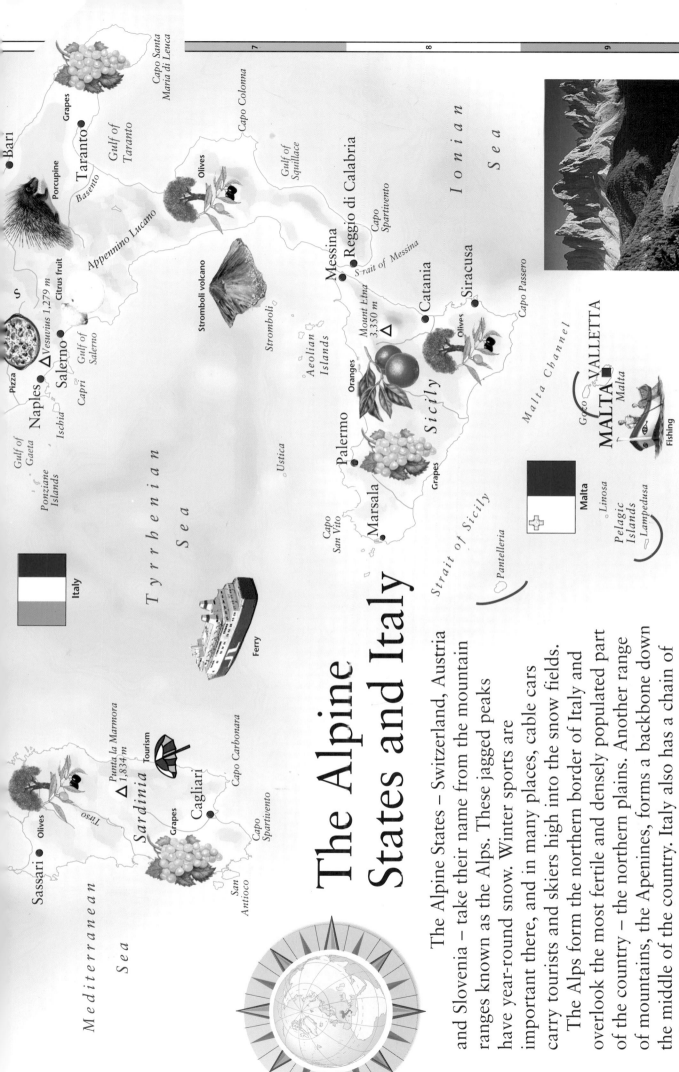

The Alpine States and Italy

The Alpine States – Switzerland, Austria and Slovenia – take their name from the mountain ranges known as the Alps. These jagged peaks have year-round snow. Winter sports are important there, and in many places, cable cars carry tourists and skiers high into the snow fields.

The Alps form the northern border of Italy and overlook the most fertile and densely populated part of the country – the northern plains. Another range of mountains, the Apenines, forms a backbone down the middle of the country. Italy also has a chain of volcanoes, stretching from Vesuvius, near Naples, to Etna on the island of Sicily. Both Sicily and Sardinia belong to Italy.

Further south still are the islands that make up the Republic of Malta.

Two independent countries are found inside Italy. They are San Marino, which lies east of the Apenines, and the Vatican City State, which is the world's smallest independent nation and lies inside Italy's own capital, Rome.

High mountains

The Dolomites are mountains that lie to the north of Italy and form part of the Alps. Snow covers these peaks all year and they are home to many glaciers.

Italy

Malta

Bari

Grapes

Porcupine

Taranto

Gulf of Taranto

Basento

Capo Santa Maria di Leuca

Capo Colonna

Appennino Lucano

Olives

Citrus fruit

Vesuvius 1,279 m

Pizza

Gulf of Gaeta

Naples

Ischia

Capri

Salerno

Gulf of Salerno

Ponziane Islands

Tyrrhenian Sea

Ustica

Stromboli volcano

Stromboli

Aeolian Islands

Oranges

Olives

Palermo

Capo San Vito

Marsala

Grapes

Sicily

Mount Etna 3,350 m

Catania

Siracusa

Capo Passero

Messina

Reggio di Calabria

Strait of Messina

Capo Spartivento

Gulf of Squillace

Ionian Sea

Strait of Sicily

Pantelleria

Malta Channel

Gozo

Comino

MALTA

VALLETTA

Malta

Fishing

Limosa

Pelagic Islands

Lampedusa

Mediterranean Sea

Sassari

Olives

Urso

Sardinia

Grapes

Cagliari

Punta la Marmora 1,834 m

Tourism

Capo Carbonara

Capo Spartivento

San Antioco

Ferry

Eastern and Central Europe

Eastern and Central Europe is a region of cold winters and warm summers. In some places, such as in Latvia, winter temperatures drop so low that the seas freeze over. Further inland, too, bitterly cold winters are usual.

During the 1980s and 1990s, many of the countries in this area underwent huge political changes. Czechoslovakia split into two separate countries – the Czech Republic and Slovakia. Nations that had previously belonged to the Soviet Union also broke away to become independent countries. These are the Baltic states (Estonia, Latvia and Lithuania), Belarus, the Ukraine and Moldova.

Poland shares its borders with seven other countries, but still has a coastline. Gdansk in the north is a major ship-building area. The Czech Republic is a small, hilly, landlocked country in the middle of Europe.

The Ukraine is the second largest country in Europe. Great quantities of wheat are grown there – it was once known as the 'breadbasket of the Soviet Union'. Hungary has plains and rolling hills. Estonia is a land of flat plains and lakes. It also has more than 800 islands.

FACTS AND FIGURES

Largest cities
Kiev 2,750,000
Budapest 1,975,000
Warsaw 1,900,000
Minsk 1,719,000

Longest river
Danube 2,858 km

Highest mountain
Gerlachovsky Stit 2,666 m

Pigs

ESTONIA

Dairy cattle

Lake Peipus

Tartu

Estonia

Lake Pskov

Gulf of Riga

Potatoes

RIGA

LATVIA

Latvia

Beef cattle

Daugavpils

Western Dvina

Churches in Vilnius

Flax

Vitsyebsk

Lithuania

UANIA

Chemical industry

Kaunas

VILNIUS

Machinery

Vegetables

Sugar beet

MINSK

Barley

Eggs

Poultry

BELARUS

Beautiful city
Prague, the capital of the Czech Republic, has been a bustling city for over 500 years. It has been a centre of culture, learning and the arts and is a popular tourist destination.

Berezina

Dnieper

Homyel

Belarus

RUSSIAN

FEDERATION

Brest

Pripet

Pripet Marshes

Pigs

Dnieper

Desna Lowlands

Common hamster

Ukraine

Wheat farming

Chernobyl

Kiev Reservoir

Industry

KIEV

Steppe polecat

Kharkiv

Donets

Titanium mining

Saint Sophia cathedral

Steel making

Industry

Lviv

Oil

Volyn-Podolian Upland

U K R A I N E

Kremenchuk Reservoir

Wheat farming

Coal mining

Dnipropetrovsk

Donetsk

Maize

M o u n t a i n s

Chernivtsi

Dniester

Sunflowers

Cossack dancers

Maize

Mariupol

Gulf of Taganrog

Southern Bug

Kakhovka Reservoir

MOLDOVA

B l a c k   S e a   L o w l a n d

Sunflowers

Sea of Azov

Hungary

Moldova

CHISINAU

Grapes

Sunflowers

Odesa

Gas

Kerch

ROMANIA

Prut

Sunflowers

B l a c k   S e a

Crimean Peninsula

Sevastopol

0   200   400 km

0   100   200 miles

Southeastern Europe

Much of Southeastern Europe is mountainous. Farmers graze their sheep and goats on the slopes, while growing crops such as grains and grapes on the lower land. The climate is changeable – winters are usually bitterly cold, especially in the north, while the south enjoys milder winters and extremely hot, dry summers. The coastlines along the Adriatic, Black and Mediterranean seas, and especially the islands in the Aegean Sea, are all popular with tourists. Bosnia & Herzegovina has the shortest coastline in the region – just 20 km on the Adriatic coast.

War has taken its toll in this area. During the 1990s, the peoples of Yugoslavia fought bitterly and divided their country into five new countries – Bosnia & Herzegovina, Croatia, Slovenia, Serbia & Montenegro, and Macedonia. Today, these countries are beginning to rebuild stable societies. Greece is a rugged country with many islands. It is also one of the oldest civilizations in Europe. Ancient cultures thrived here, and many fantastic ruins remain to this day.

Gathering roses

Agriculture is very important in Southeastern Europe and many of its people make their living from the land. Here, two young women are hard at work harvesting roses on a farm in Bulgaria.

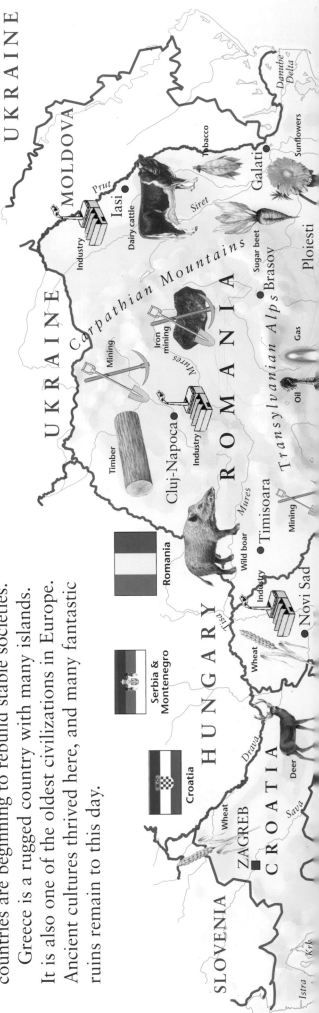

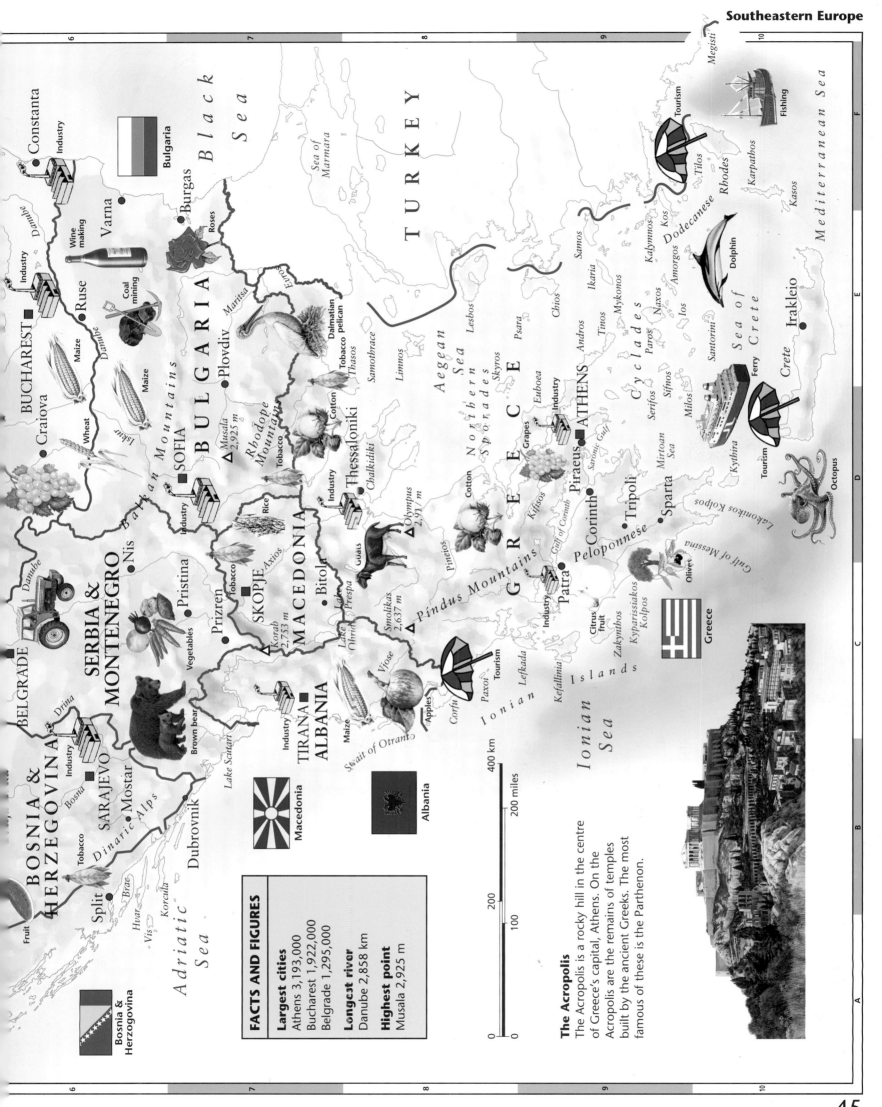

Black Sea

Sea of Marmara

T U R K E Y

Mediterranean Sea

Constanta
Industry
Danube
Varna
Wine making
Ruse
Industry
BUCHAREST
Maize
Maize
Craiova
Wheat
Coal mining
Danube
Danube
Isăr
Burgas
Roses
Dalmatian pelican
Tobacco field
Thasos
Samothrace
Limnos
Lesbos
Psara
Chios
Skyros
Northern Sporades
Aegean Sea

Megisti
Tourism
Fishing
Tilos
Rhodes
Karpathos
Kasos
Kos
Kalymnos
Dodecanese
Samos
Ikaria
Dolphin

Bulgaria

Plovdiv
Musala 2,925 m
Rhodope Mountains
Cotton
Tobacco
Industry
Balkan Mountains
SOFIA
B U L G A R I A
Maritsa
Evros

Industry
Rice
Thessaloníki
Chalkidikí
Industry
Olympus 2,917 m
Pineios
Goats
Korab 2,753 m
SKOPJE
Axios
M A C E D O N I A
Bitola
Lake Prespa
Lake Ohrid
Smolikas 2,637 m
Pindus Mountains
G R E E C E
Cotton
Grapes
Industry
ATHENS
Piraeus
Saronic Gulf
Kifisos
Corinth
Gulf of Corinth
Tripoli
Sparta
Olives
Peloponnese
Patra
Kyparissiakos Kolpos
Citrus fruit
Zakynthos
Mirtoan Sea
Lakonikos Kolpos
Gulf of Messina
Octopus
Kythira
Tourism
Cyclades
Andros
Tinos
Mykonos
Naxos
Ios
Santorini
Paros
Serifos
Sifnos
Milos
Euboea
Amorgos
Sea of Crete
Crete
Irakleio
Ferry

Nis
Pristina
SERBIA & MONTENEGRO
BELGRADE
Prizren
Tobacco
Vegetables
Drina
Damube
Industry
SARAJEVO
BOSNIA & HERZEGOVINA
Mostar
Brown bear
Bosnia
Dubrovnik
Tobacco
Dinaric Alps
Split
Brač
Hvar
Vis
Korčula
Lake Scutari
Fruit
Adriatic Sea

Industry
TIRANA
ALBANIA
Maize
Viose
Apples
Corfu
Paxoi
Tourism
Lefkada
Kefallinia
Ionian Islands
Ionian Sea
Strait of Otranto

Macedonia

Albania

Greece

Bosnia & Herzogovina

400 km

200 miles

200

100

200

100

0

0

FACTS AND FIGURES

Largest cities
Athens 3,193,000
Bucharest 1,922,000
Belgrade 1,295,000

Longest river
Danube 2,858 km

Highest point
Musala 2,925 m

The Acropolis
The Acropolis is a rocky hill in the centre of Greece's capital, Athens. On the Acropolis are the remains of temples built by the ancient Greeks. The most famous of these is the Parthenon.

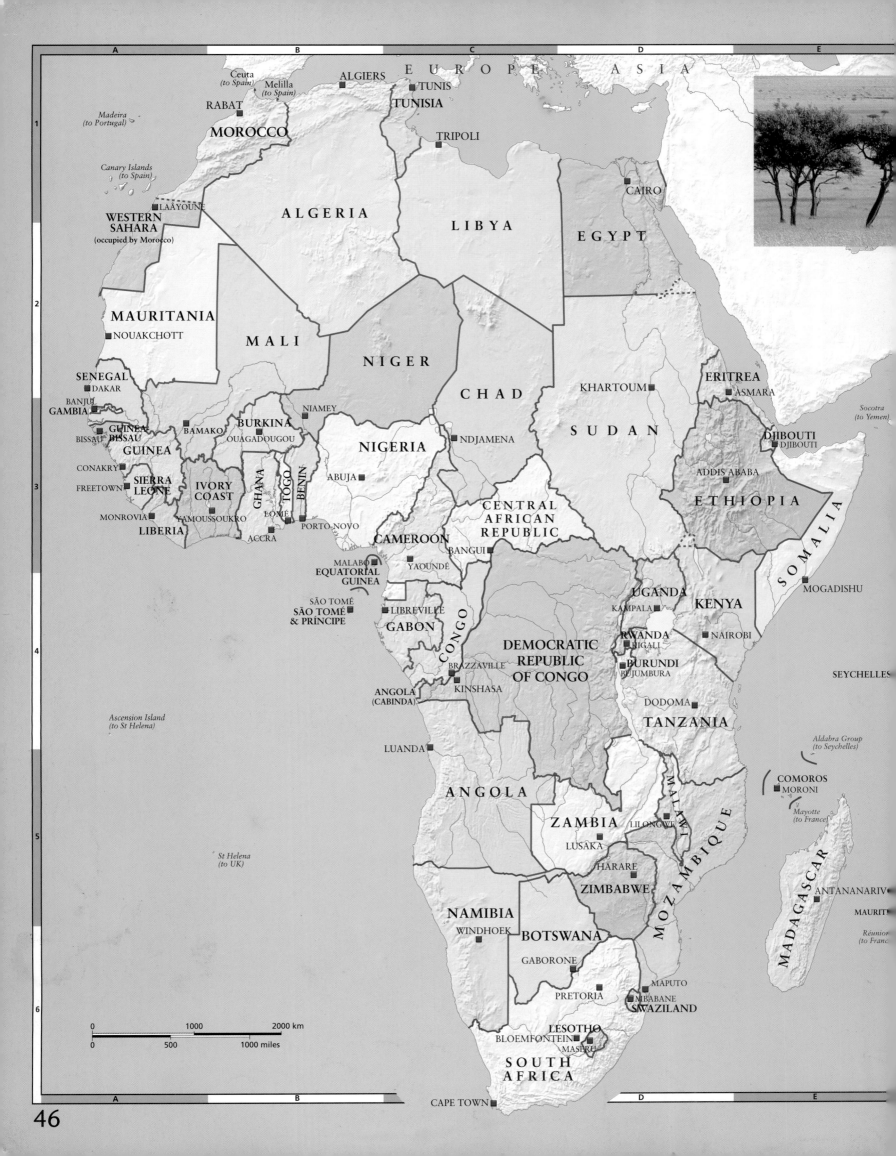

EUROPE ASIA

Madeira
(to Portugal)

Ceuta
(to Spain)
Melilla
(to Spain)

ALGIERS
TUNIS
TUNISIA

RABAT
MOROCCO

TRIPOLI

CAIRO

Canary Islands
(to Spain)

LAÂYOUNE

WESTERN
SAHARA
(occupied by Morocco)

ALGERIA

LIBYA

EGYPT

MAURITANIA

MALI

NIGER

CHAD

KHARTOUM

ERITREA
ASMARA

Socotra
(to Yemen)

NOUAKCHOTT

SENEGAL
DAKAR

BANJUL
GAMBIA

NIAMEY

SUDAN

DJIBOUTI
DJIBOUTI

GUINEA
BISSAU
BISSAU

BAMAKO
BURKINA
OUAGADOUGOU

NIGERIA

NDJAMENA

ADDIS ABABA

GUINEA

ABUJA

ETHIOPIA

CONAKRY
FREETOWN
SIERRA
LEONE

IVORY
COAST

GHANA
TOGO
BENIN

MONROVIA
YAMOUSSOUKRO
LOMÉ

LIBERIA
ACCRA

PORTO-NOVO

CENTRAL
AFRICAN
REPUBLIC

SOMALIA

CAMEROON
BANGUI

MALABO
EQUATORIAL
GUINEA

YAOUNDÉ

UGANDA
KAMPALA

KENYA

MOGADISHU

SÃO TOMÉ
SÃO TOMÉ
& PRÍNCIPE

LIBREVILLE

GABON

CONGO

DEMOCRATIC
REPUBLIC
OF CONGO

RWANDA
KIGALI

NAIROBI

Ascension Island
(to St Helena)

BRAZZAVILLE
KINSHASA

BURUNDI
BUJUMBURA

SEYCHELLES

ANGOLA
(CABINDA)

DODOMA

LUANDA

TANZANIA

Aldabra Group
(to Seychelles)

St Helena
(to UK)

ANGOLA

MALAWI

COMOROS
MORONI

Mayotte
(to France)

ZAMBIA
LUSAKA

LILONGWE

MADAGASCAR

ANTANANARIV

MAURIT

HARARE

MOZAMBIQUE

ZIMBABWE

Réunion
(to Franc

NAMIBIA
WINDHOEK

BOTSWANA

GABORONE

MAPUTO

PRETORIA
MBABANE
SWAZILAND

0   1000   2000 km
0   500   1000 miles

LESOTHO
BLOEMFONTEIN
MASERU

SOUTH
AFRICA

46

CAPE TOWN

Going green

During the wet season, lush grass grows in the Masai Mara game reserve in Kenya, and the trees burst into life. Animals, including wildebeest, gazelles, giraffes and lions, come to feast on the fresh foods.

AFRICA

Africa is the second largest continent, making up about 20 per cent of the earth's land mass. It is almost completely surrounded by water. Only a narrow finger of land at Suez in Egypt connects the continent with Asia. When seen from space, Africa looks as if it can be divided into three broad bands. The northern part is mainly covered by the Sahara – the largest hot desert in the world. The middle band lies across the Equator and is covered with tropical grasslands and rainforests. The grasslands, or savannah, are home to most of Africa's large wildlife, including elephants, rhinos, lions and leopards. Further south, the lands become drier again. The Great Rift Valley, a crack in the earth's crust, runs through East Africa. Mountains, gorges and deep lakes, including Lake Victoria, mark its course. The Nile, the longest river in the world, is found in Africa.

There are over 50 separate nations in Africa. These are home to many different peoples and cultures.

Lifeblood of Egypt

The River Nile rises in eastern Africa and flows through Egypt, towards the Mediterranean Sea. It has been a major transport route for over 5,000 years. Traditional boats, such as this felucca, still travel its waters today.

Living in Africa

There are lots of children in Africa as the population is growing fast. In many places it is difficult to provide enough schools for everyone.

Northern Africa

Much of north Africa consists of dry, arid land, where few people live. The Sahara Desert, one of the hottest places on earth, stretches over 8 million km² and covers much of the region. The Atlas Mountains fringe the desert in the northwest, and the countries here – Algeria, Morocco and Tunisia – enjoy more rains and fertile lands along the Mediterranean coasts. South of the Sahara, the land is dry and dusty, with unpredictable rainfalls, and droughts are common. This area is called the Sahel. To the east of the Sahara is the fertile Nile valley. Most Egyptians live within the Nile valley, and its capital, Cairo, is one of the busiest cities in the world.

Many of the countries in west Africa are covered by rainforests, which support a varied mix of plant and animal life. The region is also relatively rich in natural resources and minerals, and is developing industries to process them. Civil wars have taken their toll in recent times, with many countries still fighting.

Algeria

Mauritania

Souk shopping
Entertainers and traders make shopping in souks (markets) an exciting event. Here, the Djmaa El Fna square in Marrakech bustles with life.

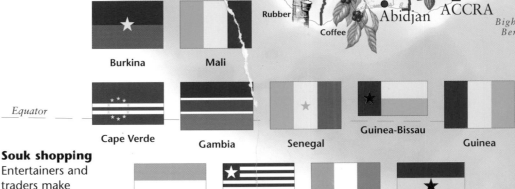

Burkina

Mali

Cape Verde

Gambia

Senegal

Guinea-Bissau

Guinea

Equator

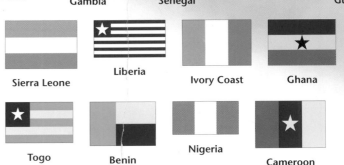

Sierra Leone

Liberia

Ivory Coast

Ghana

Togo

Benin

Nigeria

Cameroon

Map labels:

PORTUGAL SPAIN

Strait of Gibraltar

Tangier Oran

RABAT Fès Leather tanning

Morocco Casablanca

MOROCCO

Madeira (to Portugal)

Marrakech

Jebel Toubkal 4,167 m △

Atlas Mountains

Cattle

Canary Islands (to Spain)

Lanzarote

Santa Cruz Las Palmas

Tenerife

Gran Canaria Barley

LAÂYOUNE

WESTERN SAHARA (occupied by Morocco)

A L G E R

Sand cat

Iron ore mining

S a h a

MALI

Adrar des Ifôghas

Azaouâd Gold mining

Dates

NOUAKCHOTT

MAURITANIA

Timbuktu

CAPE VERDE Boa Vista

Senegal

PRAIA Santiago

DAKAR Oil refinery

Stilt-dancer

S a

Niger Cotton

NIAMEY

BANJUL GAMBIA

SENEGAL

BAMAKO BURKINA

OUAGADOUGOU

Fishing

BISSAU Bauxite mining

Benin mask

Niger

GUINEA-BISSAU

Cotton

GUINEA

Pineapple Korhogo

GHANA

CONAKRY

Diamond mining

IVORY COAST Lake Volta

Ogbomosho

FREETOWN SIERRA LEONE

YAMOUSSOUKRO

PORTO-NOVO

LOME

Kumasi Lagos

MONROVIA

Cocoa

ACCRA

LIBERIA

Rubber

Abidjan

Bight of Benin

Coffee

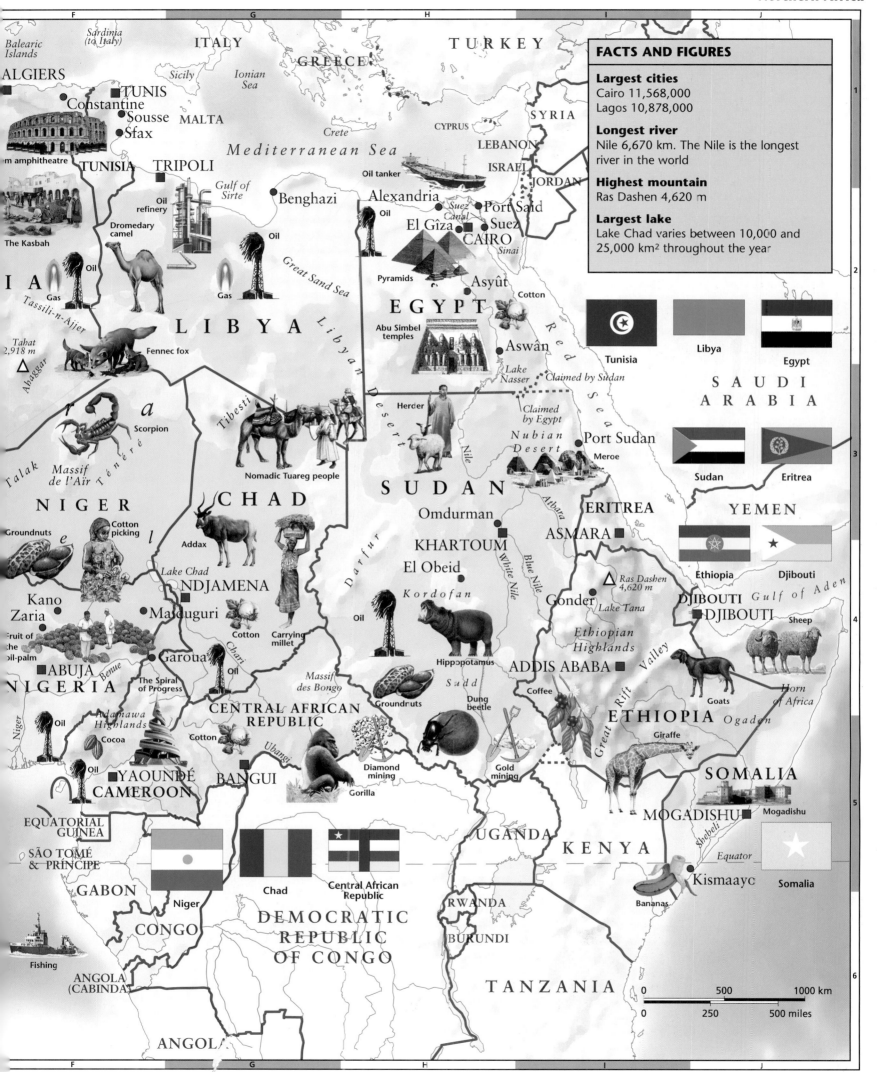

ITALY

Sardinia (to Italy)

Balearic Islands

ALGIERS

TUNIS
Constantine
Sousse
Sfax

Sicily

MALTA

Ionian Sea

GREECE

Crete

TURKEY

Mediterranean Sea

CYPRUS

SYRIA

LEBANON

ISRAEL

JORDAN

m amphitheatre

The Kasbah

TUNISIA

TRIPOLI

Gulf of Sirte

Oil refinery

Benghazi

Oil tanker

Alexandria
El Gîza
CAIRO

Suez Canal

Port Said
Suez

Sinai

Dromedary camel

Oil

Oil

Oil

Gas

Gas

Gas

Tassili-n-Ajjer

Tahat 2,918 m

Ahaggar

LIBYA

Great Sand Sea

Libyan Desert

Pyramids

EGYPT

Asyût

Cotton

Abu Simbel temples

Aswân

Lake Nasser

Red Sea

Claimed by Sudan

SAUDI ARABIA

Fennec fox

Scorpion

Talak

Massif de l'Air

Ténéré

Tibesti

Nomadic Tuareg people

Herder

Claimed by Egypt

Nubian Desert

Port Sudan
Meroe

Tunisia   Libya   Egypt

Sudan   Eritrea

NIGER

CHAD

Addax

SUDAN

Darfur

Omdurman

KHARTOUM

El Obeid

Kordofan

ERITREA

ASMARA

YEMEN

Ethiopia   Djibouti

Groundnuts

Cotton picking

Lake Chad

NDJAMENA

Kano
Zaria

Maiduguri

Cotton

Carrying millet

Oil

Hippopotamus

White Nile

Blue Nile

Gonder

Lake Tana

Ras Dashen 4,620 m

DJIBOUTI
DJIBOUTI

Gulf of Aden

Sheep

Fruit of the oil-palm

Garoua

Chari

Oil

Massif des Bongo

Groundnuts

Sudd

Ethiopian Highlands

Coffee

ADDIS ABABA

Dung beetle

Great Rift Valley

Goats

ETHIOPIA

Ogaden

Horn of Africa

ABUJA

NIGERIA

The Spiral of Progress

Benue

Niger

Oil

Adamawa Highlands

Cocoa

Oil

CENTRAL AFRICAN REPUBLIC

Cotton

Ubangi

Gorilla

Diamond mining

Gold mining

Giraffe

SOMALIA

YAOUNDÉ
CAMEROON

BANGUI

MOGADISHU
Mogadishu

EQUATORIAL GUINEA

SÃO TOMÉ & PRÍNCIPE

Niger   Chad   Central African Republic

UGANDA

KENYA

Shebeli

Equator

Kismaayo

Somalia

GABON

DEMOCRATIC REPUBLIC OF CONGO

RWANDA

Bananas

CONGO

BURUNDI

Fishing

ANGOLA (CABINDA)

TANZANIA

ANGOLA

0   500   1000 km

0   250   500 miles

49

Central and Southern Africa

Lowland covered with lush rainforests stretches across much of the centre of Africa, although the rainforests are shrinking as trees are cut down for export. Further east are vast areas of savannah, with long grasses and scattered trees. Many of Africa's well-known wild animals live around the savannahs, and thousands of tourists visit each year to see them.

A volcanic mountain range forms the borders between Rwanda, Uganda and the Democratic Republic of Congo. Bitter wars have been fought here in recent years. Further south lies a high plateau. Many of the rivers here have mighty waterfalls, such as the Victoria Falls on the borders of Zambia and Zimbabwe. These rivers are dammed for hydroelectricity. Namibia and Botswana are both dry countries with desert areas – the Namib and Kalahari. South Africa is by far the wealthiest country in Africa, with its rich gold and diamond mines.

FACTS AND FIGURES

Largest cities
Kinshasa 4,655,000
Cape Town 2,350,000
Nairobi 2,143,000

Highest mountain
Kilimanjaro 5,895 m

Largest lakes
Lake Victoria 69,500 km²
Lake Tanganyika 32,900 km²

Longest river
Congo 4,700 km

Mountain high
Kilimanjaro is the highest mountain in Africa. It is made up of three separate volcanic peaks called Kibo, Mawensi and Shira. It is so high that snow covers its peaks all year.

50

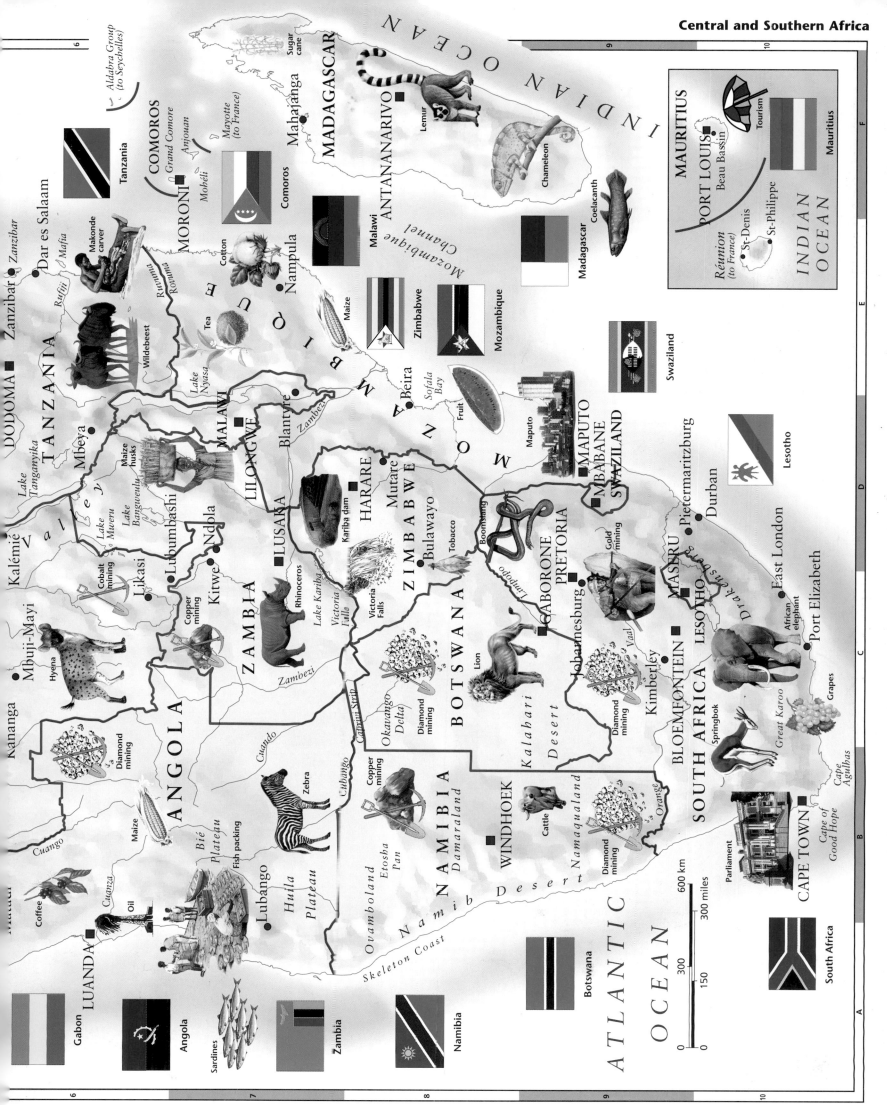

INDIAN OCEAN

Sugar cane

MADAGASCAR

Mahajanga

Aldabra Group
(to Seychelles)

COMOROS
Grand Comore
Mayotte
(to France)
Anjouan
MORONI
Mohéli

Tanzania

Dar es Salaam

Zanzibar

Zanzibar
Rufiji
Mafia

Makonde carver

Ruvuma
Rovuma

Comoros

Cotton

Nampula

Lemur

ANTANANARIVO

Chameleon

Coelacanth

Malawi

Madagascar

Mozambique Channel

Mozambique

Réunion
(to France)
St-Denis
St-Philippe

INDIAN OCEAN

DODOMA

TANZANIA

Kalémié

Mbeya

Lake
Tanganyika

Wildebeest

Tea

Maize husks

Maize

Zimbabwe

Swaziland

Lake
Nyasa

MALAWI

LILONGWE

Blantyre

Zambezi

Beira

Sofala
Bay

Fruit

Maputo

MAPUTO

MBABANE

SWAZILAND

Pietermaritzburg

Durban

Lesotho

Mbuji-Mayi

Hyena

Lake
Mweru

Lake
Bangweulu

Libumbashi

Likasi

Cobalt
mining

Copper
mining

Kitwe

Ndola

ZAMBIA

Rhinoceros

Lake Kariba

Victoria
Falls

Victoria Falls

Kariba dam

HARARE

Mutare

Bulawayo

ZIMBABWE

Tobacco

Boomslang

Limpopo

GABORONE

PRETORIA

Johannesburg

Gold
mining

MASERU

Drakensberg

East London

Port Elizabeth

African
elephant

Kananga

ANGOLA

Diamond mining

Zebra

Cubango

Caprini Strip

Okavango
Delta

Diamond
mining

BOTSWANA

Lion

Kalahari Desert

Vaal

Diamond
mining

Kimberley

BLOEMFONTEIN

LESOTHO

SOUTH AFRICA

Springbok

Great Karoo

Grapes

Coffee

Cuanza

Oil

Maize

Bié
Plateau

Fish packing

Lubango

Huila
Plateau

Cuango

Copper
mining

Ovamboland

Etosha
Pan

Damaraland

WINDHOEK

Cattle

Namaqualand

Namib Desert

Skeleton Coast

Cape
Aguilhas

Cape of
Good Hope

CAPE TOWN

Parliament

LUANDA

Gabon

Angola

Sardines

Zambia

Namibia

Botswana

South Africa

600 km
300 miles
300
150
0
0

ATLANTIC OCEAN

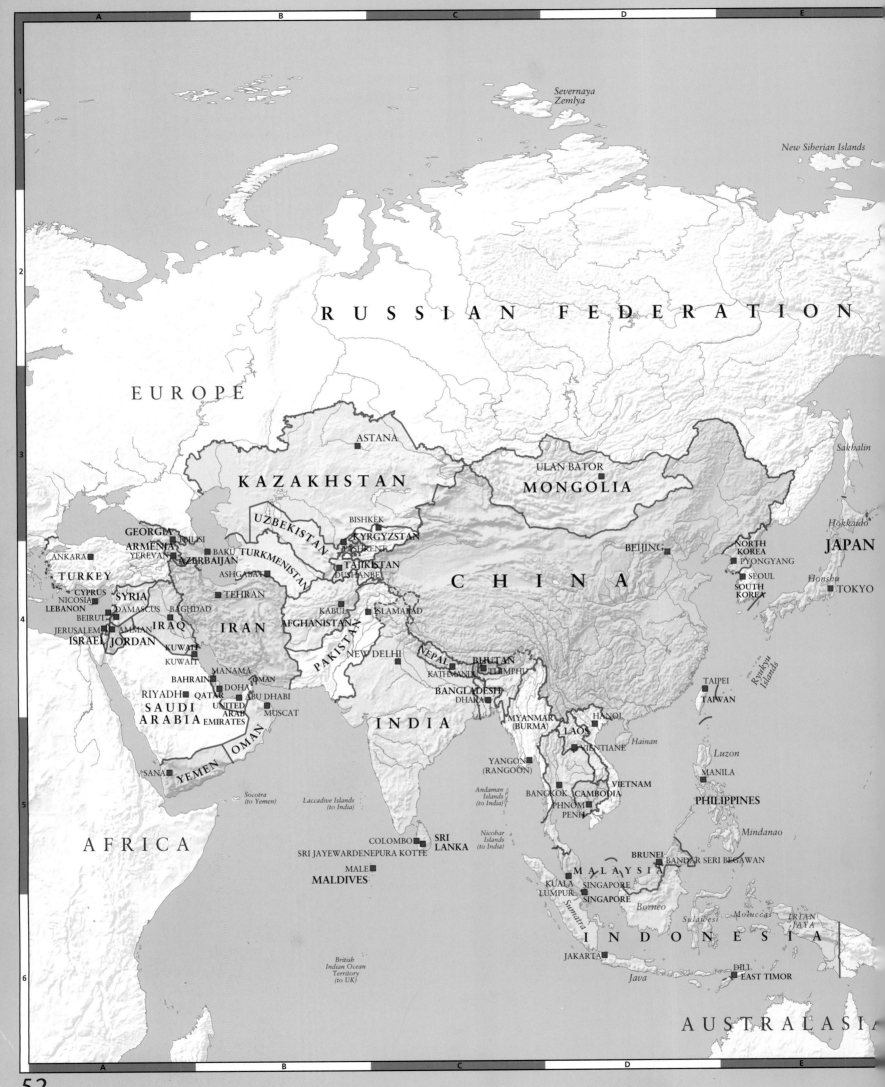

A B C D E

1

Severnaya
Zemlya

New Siberian Islands

2

RUSSIAN FEDERATION

EUROPE

Sakhalin

ASTANA
KAZAKHSTAN

ULAN BATOR
MONGOLIA

Hokkaido

JAPAN

3

BISHKEK
UZBEKISTAN
GEORGIA
ARMENIA TBILISI
YEREVAN BAKU TURKMENISTAN
AZERBAIJAN
ANKARA
TURKEY
KYRGYZSTAN
TASHKENT
TAJIKISTAN
DUSHANBE

BEIJING
CHINA

NORTH
KOREA
PYONGYANG
SEOUL
SOUTH
KOREA

Honshu
TOKYO

CYPRUS
NICOSIA
LEBANON SYRIA
BEIRUT DAMASCUS
JERUSALEM AMMAN
ISRAEL JORDAN
BAGHDAD
IRAQ
KUWAIT
KUWAIT
ASHGABAT

TEHRAN

IRAN
KABUL ISLAMABAD
AFGHANISTAN

PAKISTAN

NEW DELHI

NEPAL
KATHMANDU
BHUTAN
THIMPHU

BANGLADESH
DHAKA

Ryukyu
Islands

TAIPEI
TAIWAN

4

MANAMA
BAHRAIN OMAN
RIYADH DOHA
QATAR ABU DHABI
SAUDI UNITED
ARABIA ARAB MUSCAT
EMIRATES

INDIA

MYANMAR
(BURMA)
YANGON
(RANGOON)

LAOS
VIENTIANE

HANOI

Hainan

Luzon

MANILA

OMAN

BANGKOK
CAMBODIA
PHNOM
PENH

VIETNAM

PHILIPPINES

Mindanao

SANA
YEMEN

AFRICA

Socotra
(to Yemen)

Laccadive Islands
(to India)

COLOMBO
SRI JAYEWARDENEPURA KOTTE

MALE
MALDIVES

SRI
LANKA

Andaman
Islands
(to India)

Nicobar
Islands
(to India)

BRUNEI
BANDAR SERI BEGAWAN

MALAYSIA
KUALA
LUMPUR SINGAPORE
SINGAPORE

Sumatra

Borneo

Sulawesi

Moluccas

*IRIAN
JAYA*

5

British
Indian Ocean
Territory
(to UK)

JAKARTA
Java

INDONESIA

DILI
EAST TIMOR

6

AUSTRALASIA

A B C D E

52

Wrangel Island

0   1000   2000 km

0   500   1000 miles

Kurile Islands

On top of the world
The Himalayas is the highest mountain range in the world. The mountains stretch for 2,400 km and snow and glaciers cover many of the peaks all year.

ASIA

Asia is the largest continent. It makes up about 35 per cent of the Earth's land surface and is home to 60 per cent of the population. It stretches from Turkey and the Ural Mountains of Russia in the west to the Pacific Ocean in the east, and from the icy Arctic Ocean in the north to the tropical islands of Indonesia, with their steamy rainforests, in the south. The landscape of this vast area is varied. The world's highest mountain, Mount Everest in the Himalayas, is always covered with snow, while elsewhere, in the middle of the continent, there are huge swathes of bare, rocky desert. Frozen plains cover much of the far north. Lake Baikal, the world's deepest lake, is in Asia, together with some of the world's greatest rivers – the Yangtze and the Ganges.

Asia contains three huge and populous countries – the Russian Federation, China and India – as well as several that are not as large. It is a diverse continent, with a wide variety of peoples, beliefs, languages and lifestyles. It contains some of the world's poorest regions and wealthiest big cities.

Following Buddhism
Buddhism is one of the religions followed by millions of people in Asia. It is the most widespread religion in Myanmar and affects much of daily life there. Even children, such as this girl, can become monks or nuns.

The Russian Federation

The Russian Federation is the largest country in the world. It stretches across both Europe and Asia. Most of the people live to the west of the Ural Mountains, in the European part of the country. Large birch and conifer forests cover the region, and the River Volga brings water.

The eastern part of the Russian Federation is in Asia. This vast area includes regions of marshland and the largest coniferous forest in the world as well as the grassy plains known as steppes. Most of Russia's grain is grown on large farms there.

The Russian Federation was formed in 1991, after the earlier break-up of the communist Soviet Union. Many former states became independent countries. Under Soviet rule, industries were run by the state, and many were outdated. Today, the country is modernizing many of its industries and farming techniques.

Royal homes
The Winter Palace in St Petersburg was the winter home of the tsars (the Russian royal family). It was built in 1732CE.

FACTS AND FIGURES

Largest cities
Moscow 9,107,000
St Petersburg 4,700,000

Longest river
Yenisey-Angara 5,540 km

Largest lake
Lake Baikal 30,500 km². This is the deepest freshwater lake in the world

Highest mountain
Elbrus 5,642 m. This, in the European part of Russia, is the highest point in Europe

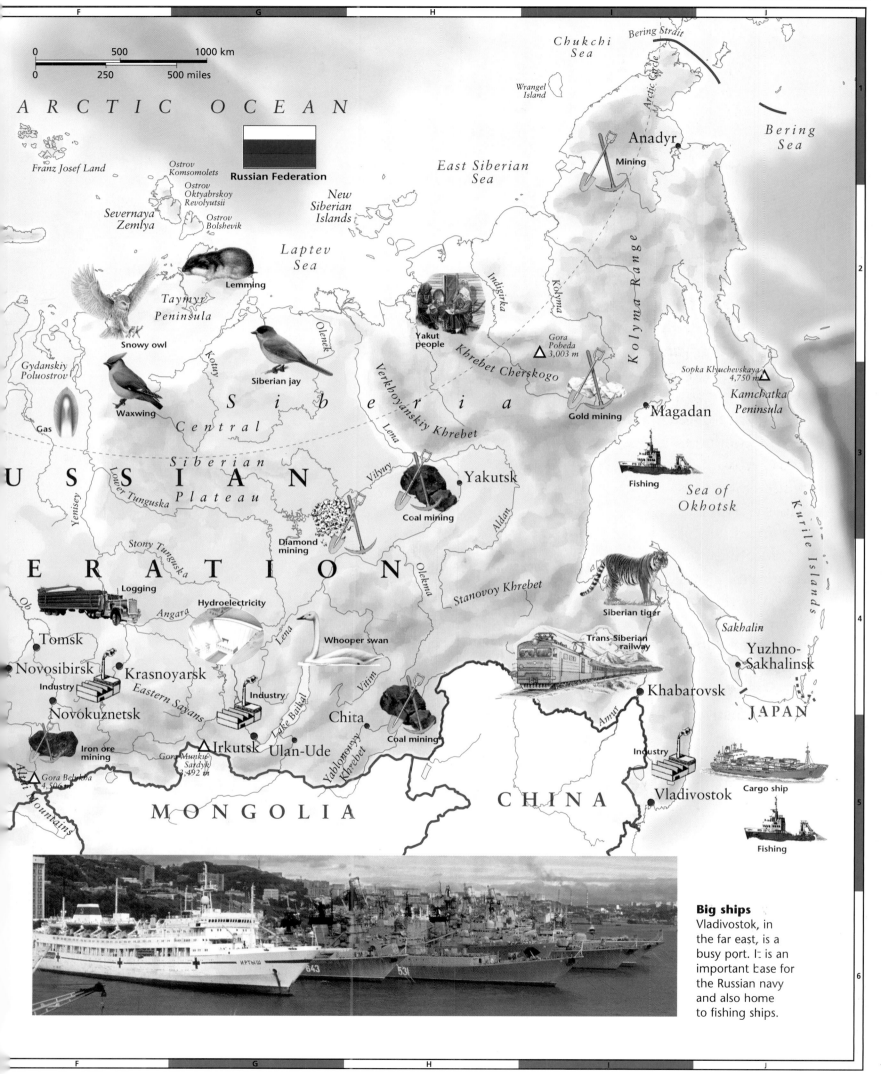

Russian Federation

0 500 1000 km
0 250 500 miles

A R C T I C   O C E A N

Franz Josef Land

Ostrov Komsomolets

Ostrov Oktyabrskoy Revolyutsii

Severnaya Zemlya

Ostrov Bolshevik

Chukchi Sea

Bering Strait

Wrangel Island

East Siberian Sea

Bering Sea

New Siberian Islands

Laptev Sea

Lemming

Anadyr

Mining

Arctic Circle

Taymyr Peninsula

Snowy owl

Gydanskiy Poluostrov

Waxwing

Gas

Siberian jay

S i b e r i a

Olenek

Kotuy

Verkhoyanskiy Khrebet

Lena

Yakut people

Indigirka

Kolyma

Khrebet Cherskogo

Kolyma Range

Gora Pobeda 3,003 m

Gold mining

Sopka Klyuchevskaya 4,750 m

Kamchatka Peninsula

Magadan

C e n t r a l   S i b e r i a n   P l a t e a u

Yenisey

Lower Tunguska

Stony Tunguska

Vilyuy

Diamond mining

Coal mining

Yakutsk

Aldan

Fishing

Sea of Okhotsk

Kurile Islands

Logging

Ob

Angara

Hydroelectricity

Lena

Whooper swan

Olekma

Stanovoy Khrebet

Siberian tiger

Sakhalin

Tomsk

Novosibirsk

Industry

Krasnoyarsk

Eastern Sayans

Industry

Vitim

Trans-Siberian railway

Yuzhno-Sakhalinsk

Novokuznetsk

Iron ore mining

Gora Belukha 4,506 m

Altai Mountains

Gora Munku-Sardyk 3,492 m

Irkutsk

Ulan-Ude

Lake Baikal

Chita

Yablonovyy Khrebet

Coal mining

Amur

Khabarovsk

J A P A N

M O N G O L I A

C H I N A

Industry

Vladivostok

Cargo ship

Fishing

Big ships

Vladivostok, in the far east, is a busy port. It is an important base for the Russian navy and also home to fishing ships.

West Asia

Three continents – Europe, Asia and Africa – all meet in West Asia, which is also known as the Middle East. It is the only place on earth where this happens, and the region has long been used by traders. The world's first cities grew up in the area between the rivers Tigris and Euphrates, about 5,500 years ago.

West Asia's northern borders are made up of mountains and seas. To the west is the Mediterranean Sea, while further south are the warm waters of the Red Sea, The Gulf and the Indian Ocean. The rivers Tigris and Euphrates bring fertility to the lands that surround them, but most of West Asia is desert or semi-desert with a climate that is mostly hot and dry. Saudi Arabia's 'Empty Quarter' is one of the most inhospitable areas on earth.

Three of the world's most widespread religions – Judaism, Christianity and Islam – have their roots in West Asia. Oil and natural gas have brought great wealth to many countries, and the region produces over one-third of the world's daily oil output. Unfortunately, both oil and religion have led to bitter conflicts. There are border disputes within Israel, which was founded in 1948 from an area called Palestine, and has been torn by conflict ever since. Thousands of Palestinians have been displaced, and want to set up their own country in their ancient homelands. Fighting continues in many parts of the region and the area is politically unsettled.

Turkey

Cyprus

Syria

Iraq

Lebanon

Israel

Jordan

Saudi Arabia

Kuwait

FACTS AND FIGURES

Largest cities
Istanbul 9,413,000
Tehran 8,900,000
Baghdad 4,478,000

Longest river
Euphrates 2,700 km

Highest mountain
Qolleh ye Damavand 5,618 m

Oldest city
Damascus, the capital of Syria, is the world's oldest continuously inhabited city, at around 4,500 years old

A place to worship
Istanbul is one of Turkey's most attractive cities. Islam is the national religion, and the city has many beautiful mosques, such as the Suleymaniye Mosque, shown.

Georgia

GEORGIA

Caucasus

Tea

Kazbek 5,047 m

Mining

TBILISI

Sturgeon

KAZAKHSTAN

UZBEKISTAN

Tobacco

Wheat

Electronics

BAKU

Oil rig

Armenia

Azerbaijan

Spinning wool

ARMENIA

AZERBAIJAN

YEREVAN

AZERBAIJAN

Lake Van

Angora goats

Lake Urmia

Tabriz

Caspian Sea

TURKMENISTAN

Wheat

Mashhad

Grapes

Cotton

Carpet making

Qolleh ye Damavand 5,681 m

Elburz Mountains

Sheep

Aleppo

Mosul

Oil

Al Jazirah

TEHRAN

Industry

Qom

Dasht-e Kavir

SYRIA

Krak des Chevaliers

Great Mosque of Samarra'

IRAN

Dasht-e Lut

Iran

AFGHANISTAN

DAMASCUS

Syrian Desert

Wheat

Samarra'

Industry

Oil

Madrasa-i Chahar Bagh

Esfahan

Iranian

JORDAN

IRAQ

BAGHDAD

Industry

Plateau

Wheat

Zahedan

PAKISTAN

Sheep

Tigris

Euphrates

Ahvaz

Zagros

Karun

Persepolis

Mountains

Bedouin

Golden eagle

Basra

Industry

Shiraz

Oil

Gas

Gecko

KUWAIT

KUWAIT

Water towers

The Gulf

Dates

Jerboa

An Nafud

Arabian

Oil

Ad Dahna

Qeshm Strait of Hormuz

OMAN

Racing camels

Gas

BAHRAIN

Dubai

Gulf of Oman

Bahrain

Medina

Peninsula

RIYADH

MANAMA

DOHA

Oil rig

Oil

MUSCAT

Hejaz

QATAR

ABU DHABI

Qatar

Great Mosque at Mecca

Riyadh

UNITED ARAB EMIRATES

Bananas

Jedda

Oil refinery

Oil

United Arab Emirates

Mecca

SAUDI ARABIA

OMAN

Masirah

Red Sea

Asir

Dates

Ar Rub' al Khali (Empty Quarter)

Gulf of Masirah

Abha

Oryx

Oil

Dates

Zufar

Sheep

Salalah

Sardines

Oman

YEMEN

Al Mahrah

Yemen

SANA

Wheat

Hadramawt

Oil tanker

INDIAN OCEAN

Coffee

ETHIOPIA

Ta'izz

Cotton

Bab el Mandeb

Gulf of Aden

Aden

0   400   800 km

0   200   400 miles

Central Asia

Much of Central Asia is mountainous, with fertile plains and rocky deserts. The world's second highest mountain, K2, is found there, in the Karakoram mountain range in Pakistan. Highlands make up much of Afghanistan and have an effect on the climate there. Northerly winds bring cold winters, but summers are hot and dry. Many of the countries in central Asia are landlocked (surrounded by other countries, with no coasts); because they are so far from the sea, their climates tend to be dry with little rainfall. Kazakhstan has cold, snowy winters with warm summers.

There are many freshwater lakes in the region, and water from these is used to irrigate crops. However, this can cause problems – so much water has been taken from the Amu and Syr rivers in Uzbekistan that the Aral Sea is drying out.

The mighty Indus river flows through Pakistan. Its waters support life along the fertile plains. In southwestern Pakistan, there are large areas of desert. Throughout history, the lands of Pakistan have been invaded and controlled by various other nations. Peaceful settlers have also made their homes here, and the population reflects this racial mix.

Traditional lifestyles

Millions of Afghans live a nomadic way of life, tending small flocks of goats and sheep. They live in felt-lined tents called yurts, which can be packed up and moved around easily.

RUSSIAN FEDERATION

Altai Mountains

Lake Zaysan

Lake Alakol

Coal mining

Gold mining

Ertis

Pavlodar

Wheat

ASTANA

Industry

Qaraghandy

Folk dancers

Lake Tengiz

Ishim

Kazakh Uplands

Lake Balkhash

Sheep

KAZAKHSTAN

Steppe

Kirghiz

Tobol

Great bustard

Mugodzhar Hills

Mining

Kazakhstan

Wheat

Ural

Oral

Caspian Depression

Atyrau

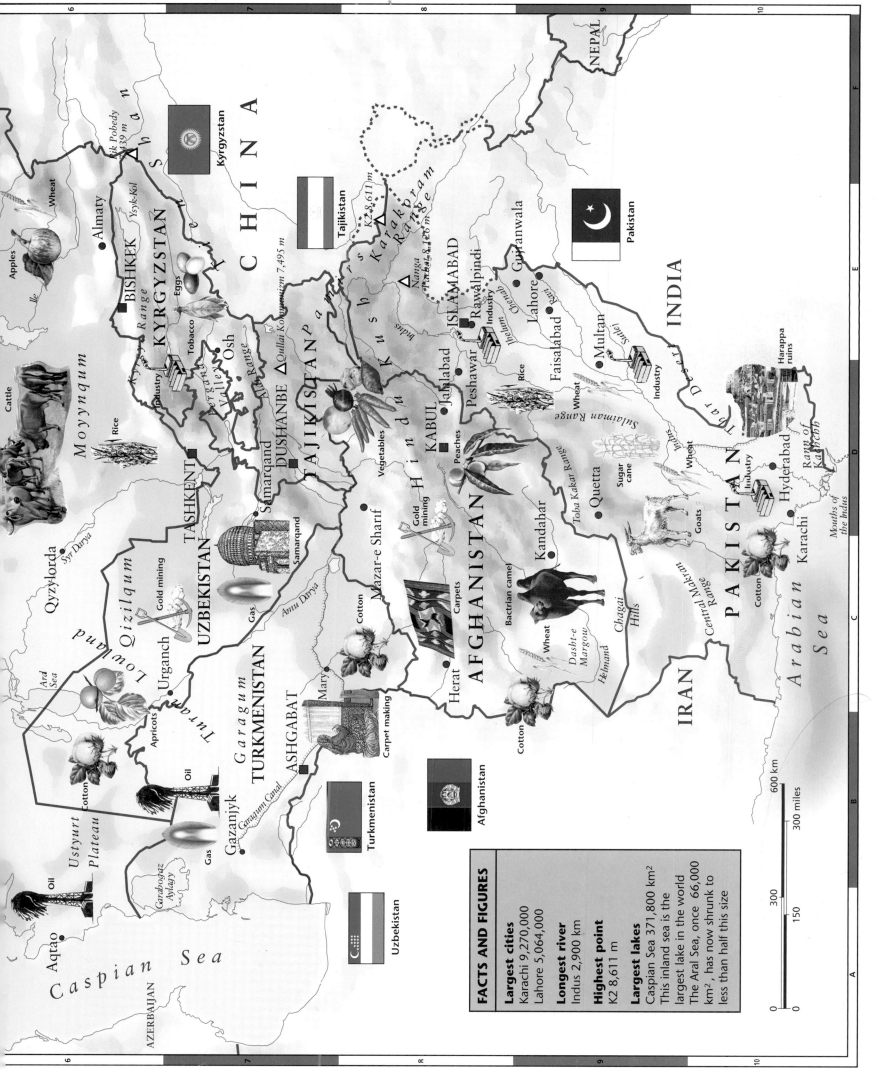

Wheat

Apples

Ile

Cattle

Moyynqum

Rice

Qyzylorda

Syr Darya

Qizilqum

Kyzyl Kum

Gold mining

Turan Lowland

Aral Sea

Apricots

Cotton

Ustyurt Plateau

Oil

Aqtao

Carabogaz Aylagy

Caspian Sea

AZERBAIJAN

Gazanjyk

Gas

TURKMENISTAN

Garagum

Garagum Canal

ASHGABAT

Oil

Gas

Urganch

UZBEKISTAN

TASHKENT

Samarqand

Samarqand

Gas

Mary

Carpet making

Cotton

Amu Darya

Mazar-e Sharif

Gold mining

Vegetables

Peaches

KABUL

AFGHANISTAN

Herat

Carpets

Cotton

Dasht-e Margow

Helmand

Bactrian camel

Wheat

Kandahar

Chagai Hills

Toba Kakar Range

Quetta

IRAN

Central Makran Range

BISHKEK

KYRGYZSTAN

Almaty

Ysyk-Kol

Pik Pobedy 7439 m

Tian Shan

Kyrgyz Range

Eggs

Tobacco

Industry

Osh

Fergana Valley

Alay Range

DUSHANBE

△Qullai Kommunizm 7,495 m

TAJIKISTAN

Pamirs

K2 8,611 m

Karakoram Range

Nanga Parbat 8,126 m

Hindu Kush

Jalalabad

Peshawar

Rawalpindi

ISLAMABAD

Industry

Indus

Chenab

Jhelum

Lahore

Ravi

Faisalabad

Gujranwala

Multan

Industry

Rice

Wheat

Sulaiman Range

Sutlej

INDIA

Thar Desert

Harappa ruins

Wheat

Sugar cane

Indus

Hyderabad

Industry

Goats

Cotton

Karachi

PAKISTAN

Mouths of the Indus

Rann of Kachchh

Arabian Sea

CHINA

NEPAL

Tajikistan

Pakistan

Turkmenistan

Afghanistan

Uzbekistan

FACTS AND FIGURES

Largest cities
Karachi 9,270,000
Lahore 5,064,000

Longest river
Indus 2,900 km

Highest point
K2 8,611 m

Largest lakes
Caspian Sea 371,800 km² This inland sea is the largest lake in the world The Aral Sea, once 66,000 km², has now shrunk to less than half this size

600 km

300 miles

300

150

0

0

South Asia

South Asia is bordered by the Thar Desert to the northwest and the Himalayas, a great chain of towering mountains, in the north and east. The Himalayas contain some of the highest mountains in the world, including the highest of all, Mount Everest. They are so high that they are covered with snow all year round, and most of the people of Bhutan and Nepal live in the more sheltered valleys to the south.

In Bangladesh, by contrast, most of the land is low-lying and flat. The mighty Ganges and Brahmaputra rivers flow through fertile valleys into the sea. Every year, monsoon rains swell these rivers and can cause terrible floods.

Much of India is covered with rolling plateau land, where farmers grow corn and millet and graze their animals. Over 60 per cent of the country's vast population makes its living from agriculture, but the country is also home to large-scale industries and huge, crowded cities. Sri Lanka is a mountainous island off the southern coast of India. It is fringed with beautiful beaches. Inland is a fertile plain, which is an important tea-growing area.

Religious river

The Ganges is a sacred river to followers of the Hindu religion. They make pilgrimages to the river to bathe in its cleansing waters. Steps, or ghats, have been built at points along its banks to help people get in and out of the water.

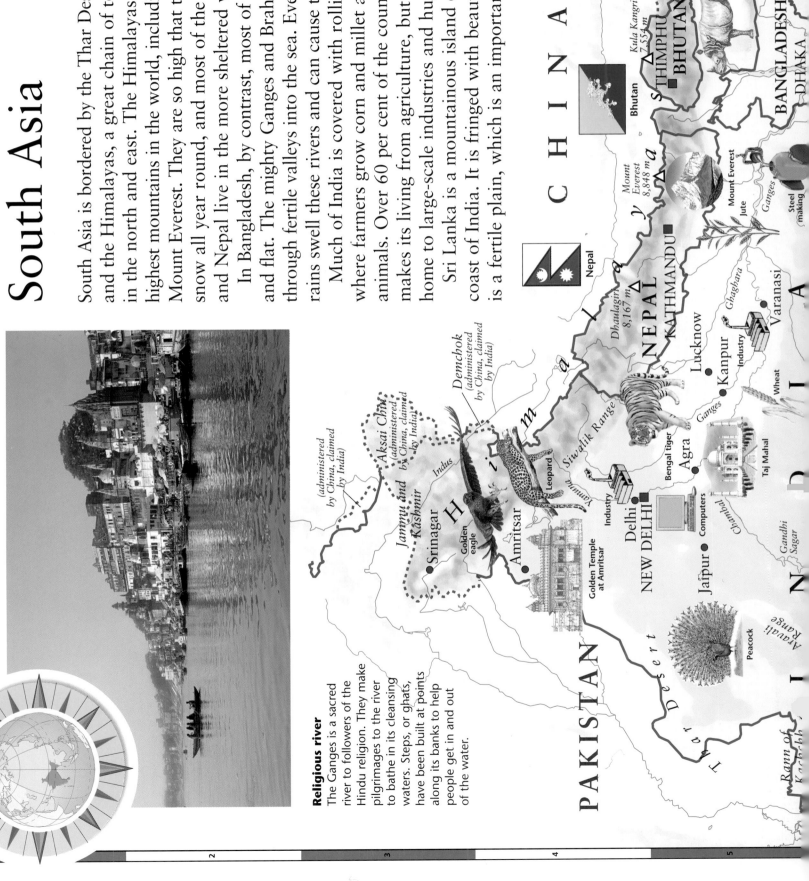

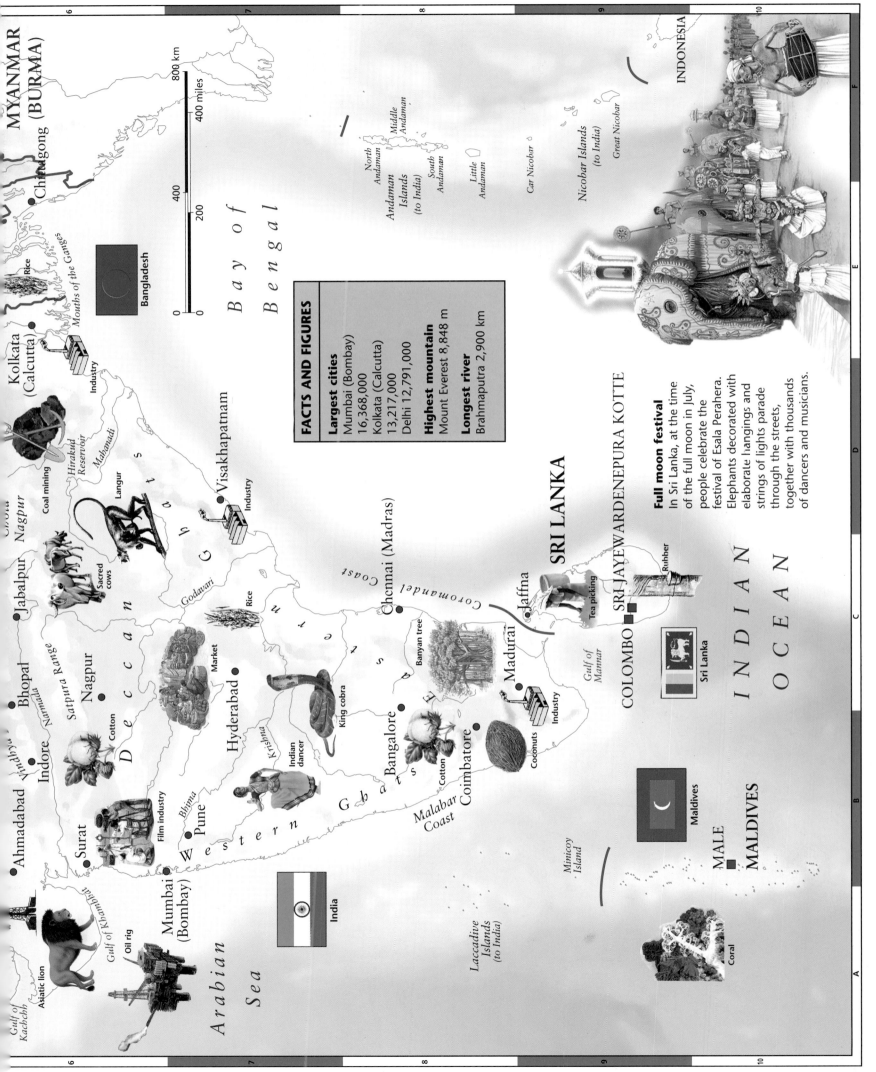

MYANMAR (BURMA)

Chittagong

Rice

Mouths of the Ganges

Kolkata (Calcutta)

Industry

Bay of Bengal

Bangladesh

800 km

400 miles

400

200

0

0

Hirakud Reservoir

Coal mining

Mahanadi

Chota Nagpur

Jabalpur

Langur

Sacred cows

Visakhapatnam

Industry

FACTS AND FIGURES

Largest cities
Mumbai (Bombay) 16,368,000
Kolkata (Calcutta) 13,217,000
Delhi 12,791,000

Highest mountaln
Mount Everest 8,848 m

Longest river
Brahmaputra 2,900 km

North Andaman

Middle Andaman

South Andaman

Little Andaman

Andaman Islands (to India)

Car Nicobar

Nicobar Islands (to India)

Great Nicobar

INDONESIA

Ahmadabad

Bhopal

Narmada

Satpura Range

Nagpur

Godavari

Rice

Market

Eastern Ghats

Chennai (Madras)

Coromandel Coast

SRI LANKA

Full moon festival
In Sri Lanka, at the time of the full moon in July, people celebrate the festival of Esala Perahera. Elephants decorated with elaborate hangings and strings of lights parade through the streets, together with thousands of dancers and musicians.

Indore

Vindhya

Deccan

Krishna

Hyderabad

King cobra

Indian dancer

Banyan tree

Bangalore

Madurai

Jaffna

Rubber

Tea picking

SRI JAYEWARDENEPURA KOTTE

COLOMBO

Gulf of Mannar

Sri Lanka

INDIAN OCEAN

Asiatic lion

Gulf of Kachchh

Surat

Oil rig

Gulf of Khambhat

Mumbai (Bombay)

Film industry

Bhima

Pune

Western Ghats

Malabar Coast

Coimbatore

Cotton

Coconuts

Industry

India

MALE

MALDIVES

Maldives

Minicoy Island

Laccadive Islands (to India)

Coral

Arabian Sea

Cotton

61

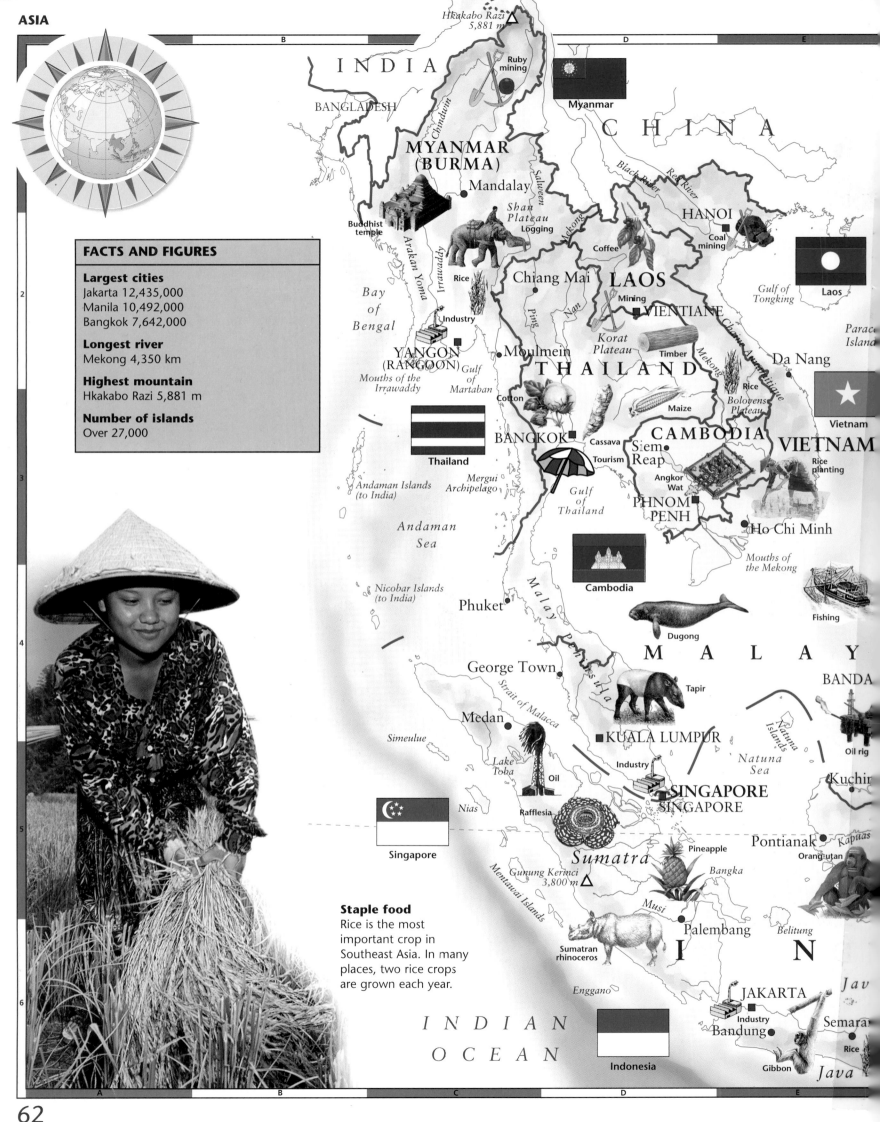

FACTS AND FIGURES

Largest cities
Jakarta 12,435,000
Manila 10,492,000
Bangkok 7,642,000

Longest river
Mekong 4,350 km

Highest mountain
Hkakabo Razi 5,881 m

Number of islands
Over 27,000

Staple food
Rice is the most important crop in Southeast Asia. In many places, two rice crops are grown each year.

Southeast Asia

Sitting across the Equator, Southeast Asia is always hot and often wet, as thunderstorms are common. High mountains and dense forests, home to thousands of unique species of plants and animals, cover much of the land. Beside the great rivers, the Irrawaddy and Mekong, are fertile plains which are important rice-growing areas.

A long, thin strip of land stretches south from Thailand into Malaysia and Singapore. South of here are the region's thousands of islands. Borneo is the third largest island on earth. Its land is divided between Malaysia, Indonesia and Brunei. Brunei is one of the richest countries in the world. Its wealth comes from oil and gas reserves. Indonesia is an island nation. It has over 13,600 islands, but fewer than 6,000 of these are inhabited. The Philippines is another island nation, made up of about 7,100 islands.

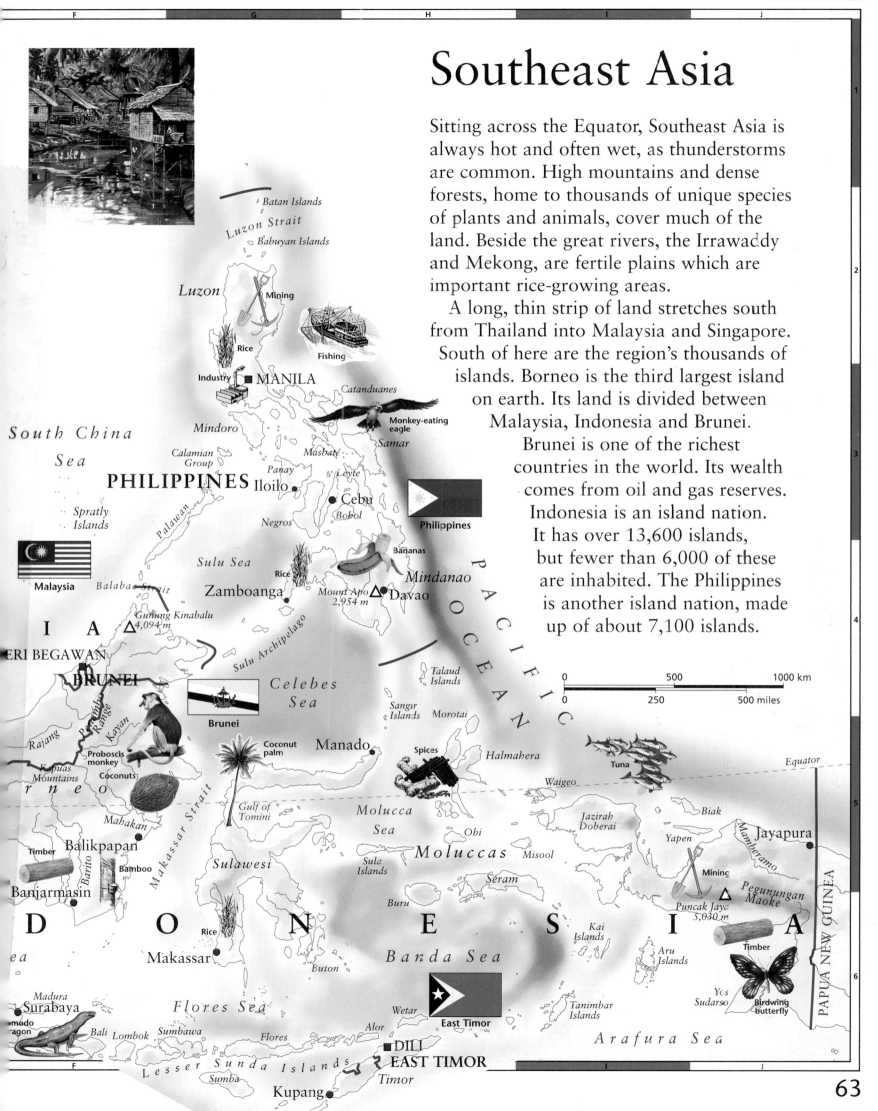

Batan Islands

Luzon Strait

Babuyan Islands

Luzon

Mining

Rice

Fishing

Industry • MANILA

Mindoro

Catanduanes

South China Sea

Calamian Group

Masbate

Samar

PHILIPPINES Iloilo

Panay

Leyte

Monkey-eating eagle

Spratly Islands

Palawan

Negros

Cebu

Bohol

Philippines

Malaysia

Sulu Sea

Rice

Bananas

Balabac Strait

Zamboanga

Mount Apo 2,954 m

Mindanao

Davao

Gunung Kinabalu △4,094 m

Sulu Archipelago

ERI BEGAWAN

BRUNEI

Crocker Range

Kayan

Rajang

Proboscis monkey

Kapuas Mountains

Coconuts

rneo

Mahakan

Timber

Balikpapan

Bamboo

Banjarmasin

Barito

Celebes Sea

Brunei

Coconut palm

Manado

Gulf of Tomini

Sulawesi

Rice

Makassar

Makassar Strait

Buton

Talaud Islands

Sangir Islands

Morotai

Molucca Sea

Obi

Moluccas

Sula Islands

Buru

Seram

Misool

Banda Sea

PACIFIC OCEAN

Spices

Halmahera

Waigeo

Jazirah Doberai

Tuna

Equator

Biak

Yapen

Mamberamo

Jayapura

Puncak Jaya 5,030 m

Mining

Pegunungan Maoke

Kai Islands

Aru Islands

Timber

Yos Sudarso

Birdwing butterfly

PAPUA NEW GUINEA

D O N E S I A

Madura

Surabaya

Komodo dragon

Bali

Lombok

Sumbawa

Flores Sea

Flores

Wetar

Alor

East Timor

Tanimbar Islands

Arafura Sea

DILI

EAST TIMOR

Lesser Sunda Islands

Sumba

Timor

Kupang

| 0 | 500 | 1000 km |

| 0 | 250 | 500 miles |

B C D E

East Asia

China fills most of East Asia. It is the fourth largest country in the world and has the greatest population – a fifth of the world's people live there. Great rivers, such as the Yellow river and Yangtze, flow across the fertile plains. Most of China's industrial cities, as well as the farming regions, are to be found in the plains, since the mountain and desert regions are so inhospitable. The rugged mountains in the southwest are home to the giant panda, which feeds on the bamboo that grows there. In the north lies the Gobi Desert, which crosses the border into Mongolia.

Hong Kong, a major financial centre, was returned to Chinese rule in 1997.

Taiwan is a mountainous country. Most of its people live in the west of the island.

FACTS AND FIGURES

Largest cities
Shanghai 9,537,000
Beijing 7,336,000
Hong Kong 6,930,000

Longest river
Yangtze 6,300 km

Highest mountain
Everest 8,848 m. This is the highest mountain in the world

Gobi Desert temperatures
Highest 45°C; lowest -40°C

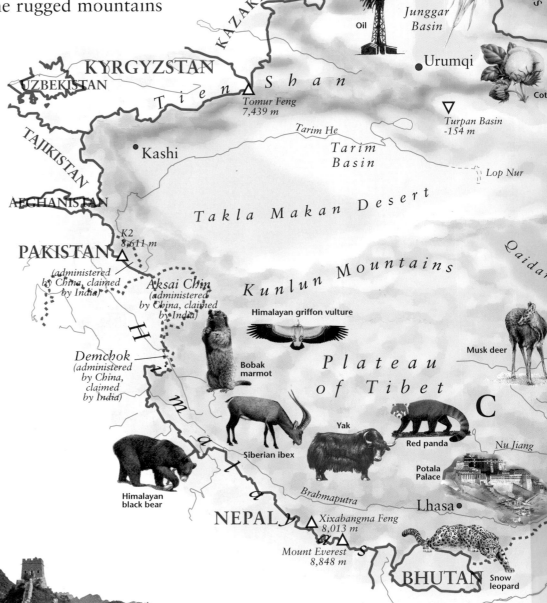

RUS

Uvs Nuur

Olgiy

Altai Mountains

Wheat

Junggar Basin

Oil

Urumqi

Cotto

KAZAKHSTAN

KYRGYZSTAN

UZBEKISTAN

Tien Shan

Tomur Feng 7,439 m

Turpan Basin -154 m

TAJIKISTAN

Tarim He

Tarim Basin

Kashi

Lop Nur

AFGHANISTAN

Takla Makan Desert

K2 8,611 m

PAKISTAN

(administered by China, claimed by India)

Aksai Chin (administered by China, claimed by India)

Kunlun Mountains

Qaidam

Himalayan griffon vulture

Demchok (administered by China, claimed by India)

Bobak marmot

Plateau of Tibet

Musk deer

C

Himalaya

Siberian ibex

Yak

Red panda

Nu Jiang

Himalayan black bear

Potala Palace

Brahmaputra

Lhasa

NEPAL

Xixabangma Feng 8,013 m

Mount Everest 8,848 m

BHUTAN

Snow leopard

I N D I A

Keep out!
At nearly 3,460 km long, the Great Wall of China is the world's largest man-made structure. It was built to stop nomadic tribes invading China.

M (

A B C D E

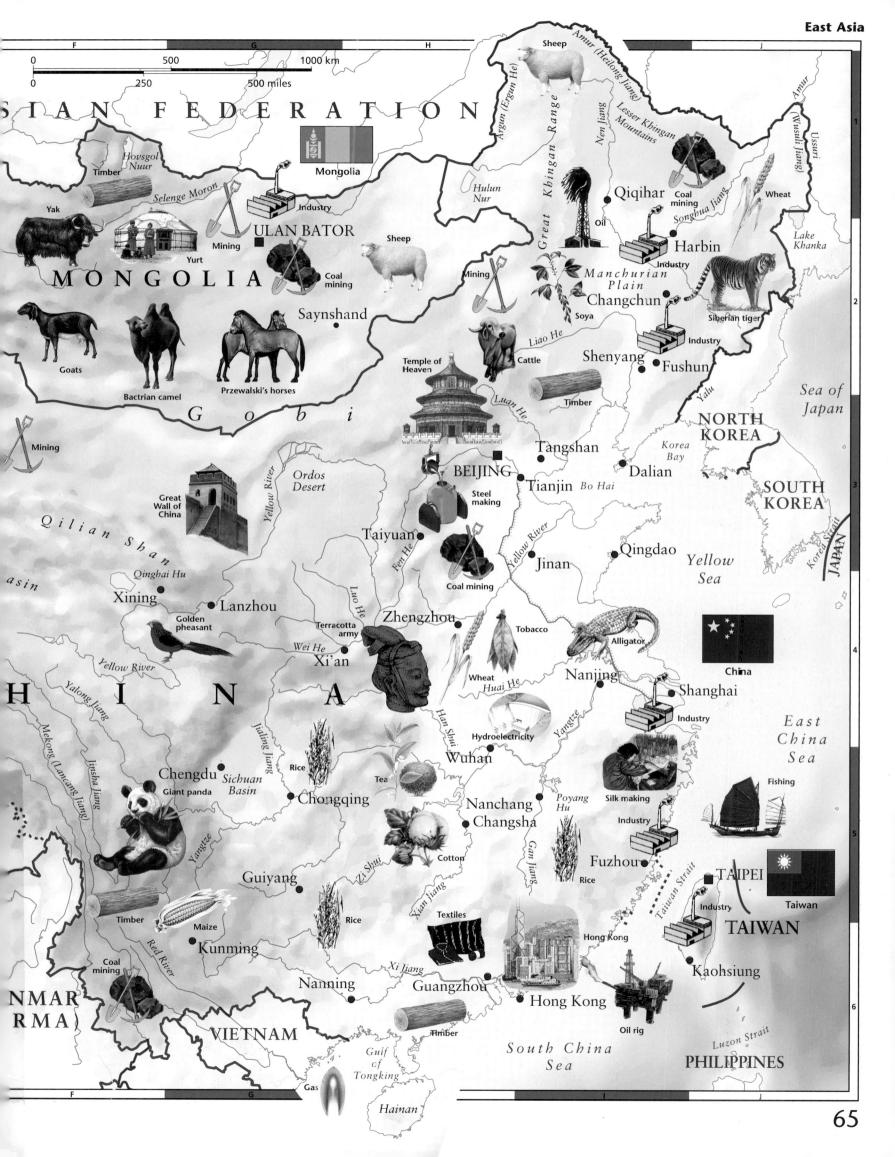

MONGOLIA

Timber
Yak
Goats
Bactrian camel
Przewalski's horses
Yurt
Mining
Coal mining
Sheep
Saynshand

Hovsgol Nuur
Selenge Moron

Industry
Mongolia
ULAN BATOR

G o b i

Mining

Qilian Shan
Great Wall of China
Qinghai Hu
Ordos Desert

Golden pheasant
Xining
Lanzhou

Yellow River

Terracotta army
Wei He
Xi'an

Yalong Jiang
Jinsha Jiang
Mekong (Lancang Jiang)

Chengdu
Giant panda
Sichuan Basin
Jialing Jiang
Rice
Tea

Chongqing

Guiyang

Timber
Maize
Kunming
Coal mining
Red River

NMAR RMA)

VIETNAM

Gulf of Tongking

Gas

Hainan

C H I N A

Yellow River

Zhengzhou

Tobacco

Wheat
Huai He

Hydroelectricity
Wuhan

Han Shui

Cotton
Zi Shui

Rice
Xian Jiang

Textiles

Nanning
Xi Jiang
Guangzhou
Hong Kong

Timber

South China Sea

RUSSIAN FEDERATION

Sheep
Argun (Ergun He)
Amur (Heilong Jiang)
Nen Jiang
Great Khingan Range
Lesser Khingan Mountains
Hulun Nur

Qiqihar
Coal mining
Oil
Songhua Jiang
Harbin
Industry
Manchurian Plain
Changchun
Soya
Mining

Cattle
Shenyang
Fushun
Siberian tiger
Industry

Amur (Wusuli Jiang)
Ussuri
Wheat
Lake Khanka

Temple of Heaven
Luan He
Timber
Liao He

Tangshan
BEIJING
Steel making
Tianjin
Bo Hai
Dalian

Taiyuan
Fen He
Liao He
Coal mining

Yellow River
Jinan
Qingdao

Yellow Sea

Sea of Japan

NORTH KOREA

Korea Bay

SOUTH KOREA

Yalu

Korea Strait

JAPAN

Alligator
Nanjing
Shanghai
Industry

China

Yangtze

Nanchang
Poyang Hu
Changsha
Silk making
Industry
Fuzhou
Gan Jiang
Rice

East China Sea

Fishing

TAIPEI
Industry
Taiwan
TAIWAN

Hong Kong
Oil rig
Kaohsiung

Taiwan Strait

Luzon Strait

PHILIPPINES

Japan and the Koreas

The islands of Japan are mountainous and rugged. About 3,000 islands form a long chain along the Pacific coast of Asia. The largest and most populated islands are Honshu, Hokkaido, Kyushu and Shikoku. Japan is in an earthquake zone and many of the islands are active volcanoes. Buildings need to be able to withstand tremors. The highest of the volcanoes is Mount Fuji, which last erupted in 1707CE.

Most of the people of Japan live in bustling cities along the coasts. But Japanese people also love nature, and celebrate it in many festivals and ceremonies. In the north of the country the climate is mainly cool, with snow in the winters. Further south, it is milder with hot, humid summers and fierce storms called typhoons in September.

North Korea and South Korea are part of a peninsula of land that stretches into the Sea of Japan. Mountains cover much of both countries. Along the coasts are plains, where most of the people live. Both North and South Korea have cold, snowy winters. The summers are usually hot and wet.

North Korea trades little with other countries, whereas South Korea, like Japan, exports goods all over the world.

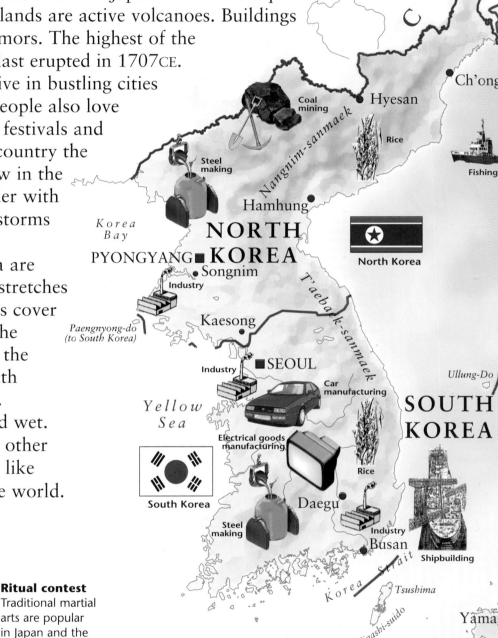

Coal mining

Hyesan

Ch'ongjin

Rice

Steel making

Fishing

Korea Bay

Hamhung

NORTH KOREA

North Korea

PYONGYANG ■

Songnim

Industry

Nangnim-sanmaek

Taebaek-sanmaek

Kaesong

Paengnyong-do (to South Korea)

Industry ■ SEOUL

Car manufacturing

Ullung-Do

Yellow Sea

SOUTH KOREA

Electrical goods manufacturing

Rice

South Korea

Daegu

Steel making

Industry

Busan

Shipbuilding

Korea Strait

Tsushima

Higashi-suido

Yamaguchi

△ *Halla-san 1,950 m*

Jeju-do

Fukuoka

Kitakyushu

Kuju-san 1,788 m

Goto-retto

Industry △

Fukue-jima

Nagasaki

Kumamot

Kyushu

East China Sea

Shipbuilding

Kagoshima

Rice

Sata-misaki

Ryukyu Islands

Tanega-shim

Yaku-shima

Ritual contest
Traditional martial arts are popular in Japan and the Koreas. Kendo, shown here, is a form of fencing that has its origins in the training of the samurai, the warriors of ancient Japan.

La Perouse Strait

Soya-misaki

Rebun-to
Rishiri-to

Macaque

Shiretoko-misaki

Kurile Islands (administered by Russian Federation)

RUSSIAN FEDERATION

Asahikawa
△ *Asahi-dake 2,290 m*
Hokkaido

Industry

Car manufacturing

Sapporo

Kushiro

Kussharo-ko

0   200   400 km
0   100   200 miles

Rice

Factory fishing

Okushiri-to

Uchiura-wan

Erimo-misaki

Hakodate

Fishing

Tsugaru-kaikyo

Shimokita-hanto

Mutsu-wan

FACTS AND FIGURES

Largest cities
Tokyo 29,950,000
This is the largest city in the world
Seoul 14,250,000
Osaka 14,190,000

Number of earthquakes
Between 800 and 1,000 each year

Number of volcanoes
Japan has over 200 volcanoes. Most are extinct (not able to erupt), but 77 are considered active (able to erupt)

Highest mountain
Mount Fuji 3,776 m

Sardines

Aomori
Hachinohe

Apples

Akita

Silka deer

Fishing

Rice

Sea of Japan

Japan

Sado-shima

Sendai

Sendai-wan

Niigata
Fukushima

Honshu

Time for tea
Each aspect of the Japanese tea ceremony is full of meaning. This ritual way of preparing and drinking tea is influenced by Zen Buddhism.

Industry

Computers

Noto-hanto

Toyama-wan

JAPAN

Kanazawa

Toyama
Nagano

Cameras

Dogo
Dozen *Oki-shoto*

Cherry blossom

Himeji castle

Wakasa-wan

Tea

Hitachi

Giant salamander

Funabashi

TOKYO
Kawasaki
△ *Mount Fuji 3,776 m*

Chiba

Gifu

Nagoya

Biwa-ko

Industry

Motorcycle manufacturing

Yokohama

Nojima-zaki

Okayama
Kobe Kyoto Nara

Industry

Hiroshima

Sakai Osaka

Ise-wan

Hamamatsu

Tuna

Matsuyama
Shikoku

Citrus fruit

Kii-suido

Bullet train

Fishing

Tosa-wan
Muroto-zaki

Shiono-misaki

PACIFIC

OCEAN

Fishing

PACIFIC OCEAN

Sagami-nada

Izu-shoto

ASIA

Micronesia

Nauru

Northern
Mariana
Islands
(to US)

Wake Island
(to US)

MARSHALL
ISLANDS

Johnston Atoll
(to US)

Pagan
Alamagan

Marshall
Islands

Palau

Saipan
Tinian

Guam
(to US)

Yap

Chuuk

PALIKIR
Pohnpei

MAJURO

Tuvalu

Kingman Reef
(to US)

KOROR

Caroline   Islands

Kosrae

Palmyra Atoll
(to US)

Babeldaob

MICRONESIA

Kiribati

PALAU

BAIRIKI

Howland Island
(to US)

Admiralty
Islands

Gilbert
Islands

Baker Island
(to US)

Jarvis Island
(to US)

NAURU

K I R I B A T I

New Ireland

PAPUA
NEW
GUINEA

Bougainville
Island

SOLOMON
ISLANDS

TUVALU

Phoenix Islands

New
Britain

Santa
Isabel

FONGAFALE

Tokelau
(to NZ)

New
Georgia
Islands

Malaita

Northern Cook Islands

HONIARA

Guadalcanal

San
Cristobal

Santa
Cruz Islands

SAMOA

American
Samoa
(to US)

Cook
Islands
(to NZ)

PORT MORESBY

Savaii

APIA

Papu New
Guinea

Espiritu Santo

VANUATU

Wallis
& Futuna
(to France)

Southern Cook Islands

PORT-VILA
Éfaté

Vanua
Levu

Niue
(to NZ)

New
Caledonia
(to France)

Viti
Levu

SUVA

TONGA

Rarotonga

Loyalty Islands

Kadavu

Lau
Group

Solomon
Islands

New
Caledonia

FIJI

NUKU'ALOFA

AUSTRALIA

Tongatapu

Vanuatu

Norfolk Island
(to Australia)

Fiji

Kermadec Islands
(to NZ)

Tonga

Samoa

Lord Howe Island
(to Australia)

CANBERRA

New Zealand

Australia

NEW
ZEALAND

WELLINGTON

Chatham Islands
(to NZ)

Tasmania

Bounty Islands
(to NZ)

Auckland Islands
(to NZ)

Antipodes Islands
(to NZ)

HAWAII
(to US)

Hawaii

Kiritimati

Islands

Marquesas Islands

Tuamotu Islands

Society Islands

Tahiti

French Polynesia
(to France)

Gambier Islands

Pitcairn Island

Pitcairn Islands
(to UK)

AUSTRALASIA & OCEANIA

Australasia & Oceania is made up of the great land mass of Australia and many thousands of islands in the Pacific Ocean. Australia itself is often described as a continent. Many of the Pacific islands were formed by underwater volcanic eruptions. Coral reefs often grow around these islands. Tropical storms, called typhoons, regularly batter these islands, and the area is also prone to tsunamis – huge waves caused by underwater volcanoes or earthquakes.

The continent is made up of 14 countries: Australia, New Zealand, Papua New Guinea and several island nations which have become independent in the last 20 years. The rest of the islands are dependencies of other countries.

Flower power
Lush plants and flowers grow in the tropical Cook Islands, and these girls have made traditional garlands called leis.

Island hopping
Of the 330 islands that make up Fiji, only 106 are inhabited. Scattered throughout the rest of the region are over 20,000 small islands, and much larger ones including Australia and New Zealand.

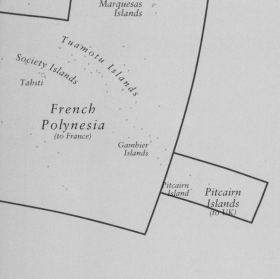

Australia

Australia is the world's largest island. Its land is mostly flat, with the main highland area being the Great Dividing Range in the east of the country. To the west are semi-arid plains where only scrub and grasses grow. Much of Western Australia is desert. In the far north, there are lush rainforests and mangrove swamps.

Despite its huge size, only about 19.5 million people live in Australia. Most of them live in towns and cities along the south and east coasts. The first people in Australia were the Aborigines, but the population is now made up mainly of people who migrated to Australia from Europe, from the 18th century CE onwards.

Australia is home to many animals that are not found anywhere else on earth. These include marsupials (mammals that carry their young in pouches), such as kangaroos, wombats and koalas.

FACTS AND FIGURES

Largest cities
Sydney 3,502,000
Melbourne 3,160,000
Brisbane 1,508,000

Longest river
Murray-Darling 3,750 km

Largest lake
Lake Eyre 9,100 km². This lake varies in size throughout the year

Highest mountain
Mount Kosciuszko 2,230 m

Famous skyline
Sydney's harbour is one of the greatest in the world. The magnificent Harbour Bridge spans the channel dividing north and south Sydney. This bridge and the Opera House are recognized all over the world.

F · G · H · I · J

Jumping around
Kangaroo mothers carry their young in a pouch on their bellies. Kangaroos travel by leaping, using their huge back feet.

Bathurst Island
Melville Island
Van Diemen Gulf
Joseph Bonaparte Gulf
Darwin
Taipan
Arnhem Land
Wessel Islands
Cape Arnhem
Gulf of Carpentaria
Prince of Wales Island
Cape York
Cape York Peninsula
Princess Charlotte Bay
Great Barrier Reef

C o r a l S e a

Daly
Didgeridoo
Groote Eylandt
Sir Edward Pellew Group
Wellesley Islands
Mitchell
Cape York Peninsula

Lake Argyle
Victoria
Baobab tree
Lake Woods
Barkly Tableland

Tanami Desert

NORTHERN

Beef cattle
Flinders
Cairns
Aboriginal cave paintings
Coral

Coral Sea

Lake Mackay
Oil
TERRITORY
Mount Isa
Thorny devil
Townsville
Sugar cane
Clown fish

Macdonnell Ranges
Alice Springs
Georgina
Sheep shearing
Cape Townshend
Coal mining
Rockhampton

T Lake Amadeus **R A L I A**
Simpson Desert
Uluru (Ayers Rock) 867 m
Uluru
Diamantina
Thomson
QUEENSLAND
Great Artesian Basin
Buckland Tableland
Bundaberg
Fraser Island

Bactrian camel
Beef cattle
Lake Eyre North
Cooper Creek
Sturt Desert
Sheep
Warrego
Koala
Kookaburra
Dairy cattle
Fishing

SOUTH AUSTRALIA
Lake Blanche
Lake Eyre South
Brisbane
Gold Coast

Mineral train
Wheat
Lake Torrens
Flinders Ranges
Lake Frome
Darling
Wheat
Duck-billed platypus
Tourism

Lake Everard
Lake Gairdner
Broken Hill
NEW SOUTH WALES
Coal mining
Steel making

lain
Port Augusta
Port Pirie
Wine
Machinery
Newcastle
Sydney Opera House

Great Australian Bight
Seal
Wombat
Lachlan
Cricket
Sydney
Wollongong

York Peninsula
Spencer Gulf
Gulf St Vincent
Adelaide
Murray
Computers
CANBERRA
AUSTRALIAN CAPITAL TERRITORY
Australia

Kangaroo Island
Fishing
Grapes
Mount Kosciuszko 2,230 m

I N D I A N
VICTORIA
Cargo ship
Melbourne
Geelong
Cape Howe
Sailing

O C E A N
Cape Otway
South East Point
King Island
Bass Strait
Flinders Island
T a s m a n S e a

0   400   800 km
0   200   400 miles

Tasmanian devil
Furneaux Group
Mount Ossa 1,617 m
TASMANIA
Hobart

New Zealand

New Zealand is made up of two large islands and several smaller ones. Much of the land is volcanic and there are many active volcanoes including Mount Ngaurahoe and Mount Ruapehu on North Island. Hot springs, pools of boiling mud, and geysers are common, particularly around Rotorua, and steam from these is used to produce electricity. South Island is dominated by the Southern Alps, which stretch down the western side of the island and are home to the country's highest mountain, Mount Cook, and the Franz Josef and Fox glaciers.

New Zealand's fertile lands provide rich pasture for millions of sheep and cattle. In fact, there are more sheep than people living there!

The first people to live in New Zealand were the Maori – settlers from Polynesia. Throughout the 19th century CE, Europeans began to move there, and they now make up about 90 per cent of the population. Most people live in the cities and coastal towns.

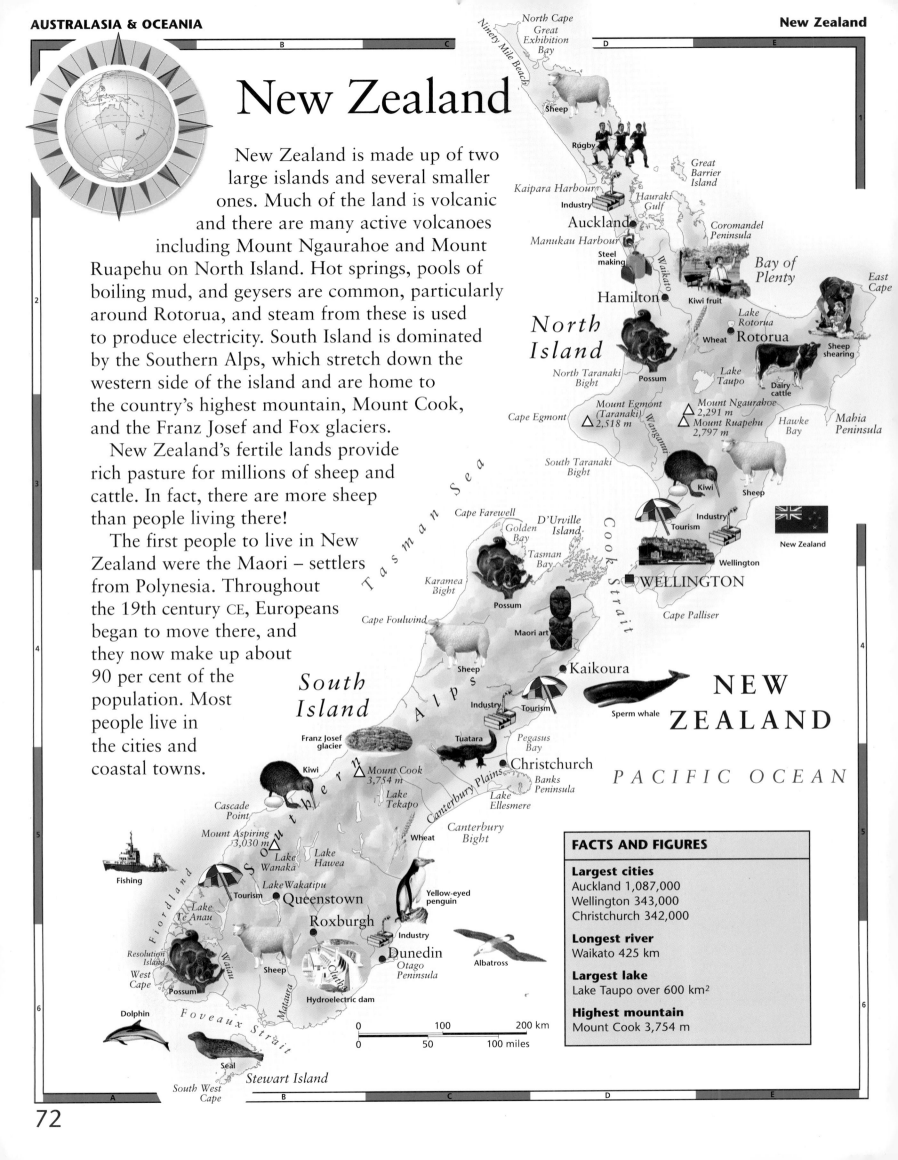

North Cape
Great Exhibition Bay
Ninety Mile Beach
Sheep
Rugby
Kaipara Harbour
Industry
Auckland
Manukau Harbour
Steel making
Hamilton
Waikato
North Island
North Taranaki Bight
Cape Egmont
Mount Egmont (Taranaki) 2,518 m
South Taranaki Bight
Great Barrier Island
Hauraki Gulf
Coromandel Peninsula
Bay of Plenty
Kiwi fruit
Wheat
Lake Rotorua
Rotorua
Possum
Lake Taupo
Sheep shearing
East Cape
Dairy cattle
Mount Ngaurahoe 2,291 m
Mount Ruapehu 2,797 m
Wanganui
Hawke Bay
Mahia Peninsula
Kiwi
Sheep
Industry
Tourism
New Zealand

Cape Farewell
D'Urville Island
Golden Bay
Tasman Bay
Karamea Bight
Cape Foulwind
Possum
Tasman Sea
Cook Strait
Wellington
WELLINGTON
Cape Palliser

South Island
Sheep
Southern Alps
Franz Josef glacier
Cascade Point
Mount Aspiring 3,030 m
Lake Wanaka
Lake Hawea
Fishing
Lake Wakatipu
Tourism
Queenstown
Roxburgh
Lake Te Anau
Fiordland
Resolution Island
West Cape
Possum
Dolphin
Southland
Waiau
Sheep
Clutha
Industry
Dunedin
Hydroelectric dam
Mataura
Foveaux Strait
Seal
South West Cape
Stewart Island

Maori art
Kaikoura
Industry
Tourism
Sperm whale
Mount Cook 3,754 m
Lake Tekapo
Tuatara
Pegasus Bay
Christchurch
Banks Peninsula
Canterbury Plains
Wheat
Lake Ellesmere
Canterbury Bight
Yellow-eyed penguin
Otago Peninsula
Albatross

NEW ZEALAND

PACIFIC OCEAN

Kiwi

0   100   200 km
0   50   100 miles

FACTS AND FIGURES

Largest cities
Auckland 1,087,000
Wellington 343,000
Christchurch 342,000

Longest river
Waikato 425 km

Largest lake
Lake Taupo over 600 km^2

Highest mountain
Mount Cook 3,754 m

The Poles
The Arctic

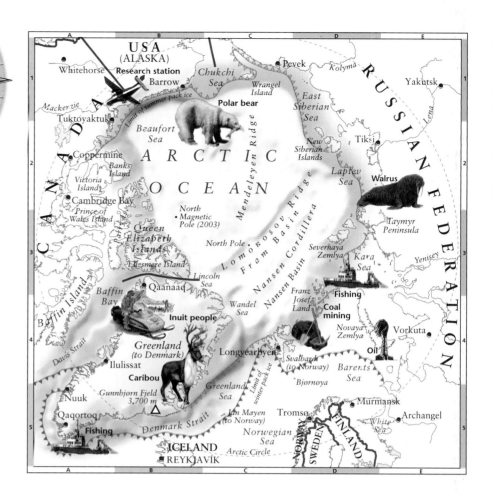

The northernmost and southernmost points on earth are called the poles. Each pole is bitterly cold and is surrounded by huge ice sheets. The North Pole floats on an ice sheet in the Arctic Ocean. The Arctic itself is an area that includes the North Pole, the Arctic Ocean and the most northerly parts of North America, Europe and Asia. During the short summers, the Arctic ice sheet shrinks, but in winter, when temperatures can fall as low as -60°C, the ice sheet grows again. Many people live in the lands of the cold Arctic, including the Inuit, Saami and Yugyt. It is also home to polar bears, caribou and walruses.

Antarctica

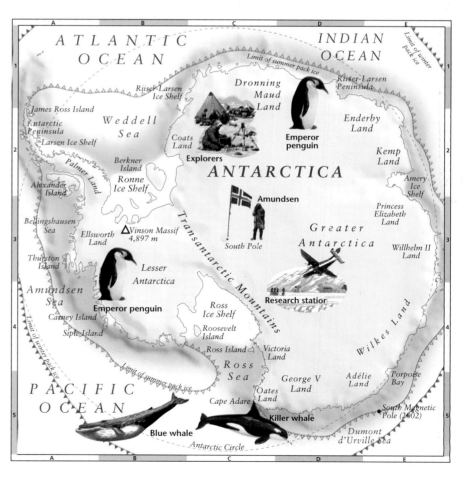

The South Pole is in Antarctica, which is the fifth largest of the seven continents. Except for a few sheltered dry valleys in the mountains the vast land mass is covered by snow and ice. Antarctica is the windiest place on earth and endures some of the coldest temperatures. Huge chunks of ice sometimes break off the ice sheets and form icebergs. These float in the water with 90 per cent of their bulk hidden beneath the waves, posing a danger to ships. There are no countries in Antarctica, and the only people who live there are teams of scientists who work at over 70 research stations that have been set up there.

FACTS AND FIGURES

COUNTRIES AND CAPITALS:
NORTH AMERICA

Antigua & Barbuda	St John's
Bahamas	Nassau
Barbados	Bridgetown
Belize	Belmopan
Canada	Ottawa
Costa Rica	San José
Cuba	Havana
Dominica	Roseau
Dominican Republic	Santo Domingo
El Salvador	San Salvador
Grenada	St George's
Guatemala	Guatemala City
Haiti	Port-au-Prince
Honduras	Tegucigalpa
Jamaica	Kingston
Mexico	Mexico City
Nicaragua	Managua
Panama	Panama City
St Kitts & Nevis	Basseterre
St Lucia	Castries
St Vincent & the Grenadines	Kingstown
Trinidad & Tobago	Port of Spain
United States of America	Washington D.C.

COUNTRIES AND CAPITALS:
SOUTH AMERICA

Argentina	Buenos Aires
Bolivia	La Paz and Sucre
Brazil	Brasília
Chile	Santiago
Colombia	Bogotá
Ecuador	Quito
Guyana	Georgetown
Paraguay	Asunción
Peru	Lima
Surinam	Paramaribo
Uruguay	Montevideo
Venezuela	Caracas

COUNTRIES AND CAPITALS:
EUROPE

Albania	Tirana
Andorra	Andorra la Vella
Austria	Vienna
Belarus	Minsk
Belgium	Brussels
Bosnia & Herzegovina	Sarajevo
Bulgaria	Sofia
Croatia	Zagreb
Czech Republic	Prague
Denmark	Copenhagen
Estonia	Tallinn
Finland	Helsinki
France	Paris
Germany	Berlin
Greece	Athens
Hungary	Budapest
Iceland	Reykjavik
Italy	Rome
Latvia	Riga
Liechtenstein	Vaduz
Lithuania	Vilnius
Luxembourg	Luxembourg
Macedonia	Skopje
Malta	Valletta
Moldova	Chisinau
Monaco	Monaco
Netherlands	Amsterdam and The Hague
Norway	Oslo
Poland	Warsaw
Portugal	Lisbon
Republic of Ireland	Dublin
Romania	Bucharest
Russian Federation	Moscow
San Marino	San Marino
Serbia & Montenegro	Belgrade
Slovakia	Bratislava
Slovenia	Ljubljana
Spain	Madrid
Sweden	Stockholm
Switzerland	Bern
Ukraine	Kiev
United Kingdom	London
Vatican City	Vatican City

COUNTRIES AND CAPITALS:
AFRICA

Algeria	Algiers
Angola	Luanda
Benin	Porto-Novo
Botswana	Gaborone
Burkina	Ouagadougou
Burundi	Bujumbura
Cameroon	Yaoundé
Cape Verde	Praia
Central African Republic	Bangui
Chad	Ndjamena
Comoros	Moroni
Congo	Brazzaville
Democratic Republic of Congo	Kinshasa
Djibouti	Djibouti
Egypt	Cairo
Equatorial Guinea	Malabo
Eritrea	Asmara
Ethiopia	Addis Ababa
Gabon	Libreville
Gambia	Banjul
Ghana	Accra
Guinea	Conakry
Guinea-Bissau	Bissau
Ivory Coast	Yamoussoukro
Kenya	Nairobi
Lesotho	Maseru
Liberia	Monrovia
Libya	Tripoli
Madagascar	Antananarivo
Malawi	Lilongwe
Mali	Bamako
Mauritania	Nouakchott
Mauritius	Port Louis
Morocco	Rabat
Mozambique	Maputo
Namibia	Windhoek
Niger	Niamey
Nigeria	Abuja
Rwanda	Kigali
São Tomé & Príncipe	São Tomé
Senegal	Dakar
Seychelles	Victoria
Sierra Leone	Freetown